MATRIX PATH OF NEO

PROGENY AND POTENTIALS

NEO

The game follows the path of the One, the messiah who realized his potential and ended the war between humankind and the machines as seen in the hit <u>Matrix</u> film trilogy. The game expands on key events and battles seen in the three films, and recreates familiar locations. Players have the opportunity to guide Neo through his path, making all of the decisions and finding new ways to solve the same problems Neo faced, or to win battles he might have failed and brave new challenges Neo never experienced.

Neo is the hacker alias of Thomas Anderson, a quiet programmer who lives two lives; in one life he goes to work at a successful software company, he pays his taxes and takes out his landlady's garbage. In his other life, he uses computers to bend the rules of society and, eventually, the laws of reality.

Providence catches up to Neo when a rebel faction led by the enigmatic Morpheus contacts him. Soon after meeting with Morpheus' second in command, Trinity, Neo has a nightmarish brush with Agents sent to interrogate him. Morpheus then leads Neo to an abandoned tenement building and offers him an important choice; Neo can take a blue pill and forget everything that has happened, or take a red pill and learn the answers to the questions that have been plaguing his mind. Upon taking the red pill, Neo learns the nature of the Matrix and the cruel design of the machines that endeavor to enslave mankind.

Morpheus chose Neo because he believes that Neo is the One, a person prophesied to be capable of changing or controlling the Matrix with his sheer will. Whether or not Neo is the One depends on his abilities to master combat and fight the overwhelming forces of the Matrix.

By progressing through the game, Neo gains greater Focus and his combat skills improve. Neo overcomes a major hurdle halfway through the game when he begins to believe that he is the One, and by using his newfound belief to defeat the Agents of the Matrix. As the One, Neo must use his abilities to determine how to override the Matrix and defeat his persistent nemesis, the ever propagating Agent Smith. This is the <u>The Matrix: Path of Neo</u>.

MORPHEUS

Morpheus is the captain of the Nebuchadnezzar, a ship that travels through the lower layers of the Earth using electromagnetism as propulsion. His crew at the start of the game includes Trinity, Apoc, Switch, and the Operator. Morpheus contacts Neo and frees him from the Matrix because he believes that Neo is the One. He serves as a mentor figure to Neo, and his fervent belief in the prophecy helps Neo to start using his amazing abilities. Morpheus appears in several levels of the game, as both training obstacle and as fighting sidekick. He is capable of utilizing almost any weapon with extreme mastery. His hand-to-hand combat skill allows him to go toe-to-toe even with Agents, although his abilities are not quite as great as Neo's.

TRINITY

As her name indicates, Trinity completes the trio of main characters, including Morpheus and Neo. She is second in command onboard the Nebuchadnezzar, and, as predicted by the Oracle, she falls in love with the One, who is Neo. Trinity appears in several levels of the game and fights alongside Neo, providing backup and support both during his training and when fighting in the Matrix. Her help is invaluable in the Rooftop Assault level, where she flanks and shoots Agents while Neo performs a Bullet Dodge. Like Morpheus, Trinity is trained in the use of most weapons encountered in the game. Her shooting is extremely accurate, and she attacks enemies as fervently as the player.

APOC

Apoc is another crewmember onboard the Nebuchadnezzar, ranking slightly below Trinity in seniority. After escorting Neo to see the Oracle, he fights alongside Neo to try and escape the trap set at the old hotel. His skill with weapons is very good, but he uses very little hand-to-hand. Be sure to cover and protect Apoc while fighting in the same area.

SWITCH

Switch is a crewmember of the Nebuchadnezzar, ranking the same as Apoc. She has a sharp personality, but is extremely efficient and fights to the death for Morpheus' beliefs. Switch is highly accurate when firing a weapon, but like Apoc she rarely resorts to hand-to-hand combat.

THE OPERATOR & LINK

Born free outside of the Matrix in the real world, 'The Operator' assists rebels like Neo, Morpheus and Trinity as they fight to survive in the Matrix. In training simulations, the Operator can be heard like a voice inside Neo's head. In the Matrix, the Operator can only be contacted through the use of a cell phone or hard line. While the rebels explore inside the Matrix, Operators view the code and look for weaknesses, building schematics, and extraction points. Listen carefully to the Operator for clues as to how to proceed and navigate while playing.

BALLARD

Ballard is the captain of the Icarus. Like most other captains he is skeptical of Morpheus' beliefs and whether or not Neo is the One. After escaping the captains' meeting, Ballard requires Neo's help to get out of a tough spot, as he is trapped inside a restaurant unable to escape while Agents close in. Ballard picks up and uses all types of weapons, and fights as well as Morpheus in hand-to-hand combat.

NIOBE

Niobe is the fierce captain of the Logos, another ship in Zion's fleet. She is also Morpheus' former flame. She is a formidable pilot and a master of weaponry and martial arts. While she can shoot accurately with any firearm, Niobe prefers to engage enemies in hand-to-hand combat. Following the interrupted captains' meeting, Niobe attempts to flee into the sewer but is surrounded. Neo must help Niobe break out of the sewer junction. Be sure to stick close to her in the initial moments of the level so that she is not overwhelmed and killed.

ROLAND

Roland is captain of the Hammer, a ship in Zion's fleet. Of all the captains he is the most fervently in denial of Neo's abilities and the most vocal in opposition to Morpheus' plans. In spite of his contrary opinions, he can tell friend from foe and will fight to the death to defend Zion, the last human city. Following his escape from the captains' meeting, Roland becomes pinned down in a warehouse and requires Neo's help to escape. Although Roland is capable of hand-to-hand, he prefers to fight at long range with machine guns and other heavy weaponry. For this reason he often becomes a sitting target. Neo must work quickly to clear an escape route for Roland to prevent him from being killed.

SERAPH

The Oracle's guardian, Seraph is an 'Exile' program, existing within the Matrix but free from its control. After being freed by the Merovingian, he served as a hound for the elitist Frenchman for some time thereafter. Following some sort of altercation, Seraph quit the Merovingian's service and became the Oracle's bodyguard. In hand-to-hand combat, Seraph is a powerful fighter on par even with Neo. Before leading visitors to the Oracle, he challenges them to a fight. During the course of the fight, he is able to determine the proper identity of the person and determine whether or not he should let them see the Oracle. Therefore, Neo must fight Seraph in order to speak with the Oracle.

THE KEY MAKER

The Key Maker is an Exile program who was accidentally freed when the Matrix was completed. He has since been captured and held by the Merovingian. He carries a ring of keys that enable him to open any door within the Matrix. Therefore, he is able to unlock the door so that Neo may enter the Source of the Matrix and deactivate it. While attempting to free the Key Maker, Neo must protect the Key Maker from being absorbed by the persistent Agent Smith.

PROGRAMS
CONTROLLING
PROGRAMS
AGENTS

Neo encounters a variety of enemies and opponents while venturing through the Matrix. Many of them take the form of human Security Guards and Policemen who typically use firearms to try and suppress Neo. Other foes are powerful programs devised by the Matrix and by other programs working within the Matrix, thus 'programs controlling programs'. Learning to identify enemies is important in determining how best to defeat them.

This chapter includes all forms of enemies encountered except for unique "boss" enemies. Bosses are identified during the game by a special health bar displayed on the right side of the screen. When fighting a boss, please refer to the proper section in the "Path of the One" chapter farther back in the book.

| AGENT | AGENT | AGENT |
| BROWN | JONES | WHITE |

SPECIAL ABILITIES	STAGE APPEARANCE
BULLET DODGE	Ever Had a Dream, Neo?
POSSESSION	They're Coming for You, Neo
FIST BOUQUET	He's Heading for the Street
	Storming the Drain
	Rooftop Assault
	Helicopter Rescue
	I Need an Exit
	He is the One
	Redpill Rescue

The Agents are the eyes and ears of the Matrix. When the laws of physics constructed to uphold the illusion of the Matrix are broken, the Agents appear and attempt to correct the situation by any means necessary--including the elimination of any witnesses. The Agents seek to capture and eliminate any rebel forces of Zion for seeking to overthrow the Matrix and free the humans from the machines. Initially, the three Agents encountered are Smith, Jones and Brown. Agent Smith is the leader of the trio, and the most powerful. After Smith is destroyed when Neo realizes he is the One, Agent White joins the trio as a replacement. Agents are armed with Agent Pistols, the most powerful handgun in the game.

At the outset of the game, Agents are nearly invincible. Their strength and speed make them almost impossible to fight, and most rebels absolutely cannot kill them. Agents are immune to handgun fire due to their 'bullet dodge' ability. In hand-to-hand, they can block most punches and kicks. Even if someone manages to kill or outrun an Agent, these foes have the ability to leap from person to person, 'possessing' any non-rebel civilian who remains plugged in to the Matrix. While an Agent is taking possession of a human, they are vulnerable to gunfire.

Once an Agent has identified a rebel, the program will stop at nothing to kill its target. Agents may even shoot Police officers or Soldiers who get in the way. With no sense of self-preservation, Agents might jump off ledges, crash through windows, destroy the environment and may even detonate nearby explosives.

Neo can defeat Agents during the opening dream sequence, but then not again until he becomes the One. Use Evade moves to avoid the strikes and grapples of an Agent. If Neo becomes stunned, use an Evade move to break the spell. Otherwise an Agent might seize Neo and commence an unbreakable "Fist Bouquet" combo. Use Focus to avoid shots fired by an Agent while attempting to move in close. Once an Agent holsters his weapon, engage him in martial arts and frequently use Focus to inflict damage and use grapple moves. Agents are especially susceptible to grenades and other types of explosions or environmental hazards.

UPGRADED AGENTS

AGENT
JACKSON

AGENT
JOHNSON

AGENT
THOMPSON

SPECIAL ABILITIES
BULLET DODGE
POSSESSION
FIST BOUQUET

To confront the threat of the One, the Architect attempts to balance the equation by creating new, Upgraded Agents. These are the Agents who appear in the film <u>The Matrix Reloaded</u> and in the second half of <u>The Matrix: Path of Neo</u>. Their names are Agent Johnson, Agent Jackson, and Agent Thompson. Upgraded Agents can still be defeated by 'the One', but they are even more powerful in hand-to-hand combat and more accurate with firearms than their predecessors. Use the same strategies employed against the previous trio of Agents to defeat them in hand-to-hand combat.

AGENT SMITH

SPECIAL ABILITIES

- BULLET DODGE
- POSSESSION
- FIST BOUQUET
- SMITH COPY

STAGE APPEARANCE

- Ever Had a Dream, Neo?
- They're Coming for You, Neo
- He's Heading for the Street
- Helicopter Rescue
- I Need an Exit
- He is the One
- The Burly Brawl
- Tuned Out
- Ministry of Smiths
- Taking the Floor
- Mr. Anderson, Welcome Back
- Aerial Battle
- This is My World

Agent Smith is the leader of the first trio of Agents that appears from the start of the game. Vindictive, sadistic and hateful, he detests everything about the human race. In every conceivable way, he is Neo's opposite. Smith cannot be defeated until Neo realizes that he is the One. Until that point, avoid fighting Smith and the other Agents altogether. Use grenades, shoot them with the helicopter Gatling gun, or throw Smith under a moving train.

After Neo realizes he is the One and defeats Smith, this super Agent enters a new phase. Unplugged from the Matrix but not deleted, Smith discovers a way to possess more than one person at a time. He becomes able to possess even unplugged rebels and other Agents. Using this method, he intends to "copy" himself enough times to take over the Matrix. At this stage, Smith becomes slightly more powerful in hand-to-hand combat. He becomes able to create copies of himself using any nearby civilians, and can use his newfound "Smith Copy" ability to drain Neo's health.

In the final stage of the game, Smith has replicated himself enough times to take over the Matrix. He becomes as fast, as powerful and just as adept as Neo, presenting a huge challenge. He also gains the ability to fly and fight in mid-air, forcing half the battle to take place off the ground.

Always use plenty of Focus when fighting Smith, if only to slow the battle down enough to anticipate his strikes and block them. While Smith attacks, use Evade moves to maneuver behind him and attack. During flight battles, use the special controls defined at the start of the stage to combat Smith until the battle returns to solid ground.

In situations where multiple Smiths surround Neo, use multi-opponent fighting moves and staff combinations to defeat them quickly. Smiths in Smith Crowds are much easier to defeat than lone, boss-version Smiths.

AXE GANG MEMBER

Chinese martial artists of the old world, Axe Gang Members never retreat from battle. They're simple programs designed to teach Neo the basics of fighting during a training exercise. Gang Members dressed in black are programmed to rush at Neo and fight, either with or without an Axe Gang Axe or Short Stick in hand. Gang Members dressed in suave green suits are programmed to take positions on the outer edges of the room, where they target and attempt to strike Neo with thrown axes. Engage Axe Gang members with hand-to-hand combat and the provided Bo Staff to defeat them. Use multi-opponent tactics when surrounded, and use Weapon Strip moves to take Axe Gang Members' axes as your own tool.

SPECIAL ABILITIES

NONE

STAGE APPEARANCE

Aerial Training

SWORDSMAN

The Swordsman is a character from the sword training program designed to help Neo hone his melee weapon abilities. He appears to be inspired by characters that appear in Japanese anime films such as <u>Ninja Scroll</u>. During this attack, he focuses his energy on his blade and then lashes out with a powerful thrust. This is a modified Killing Blow move capable of knocking Neo to the ground. He can also blind Neo by reflecting the sun's light from his sword. While Neo is blinded, the screen is temporarily filled with light. The swordsman often uses this attack if Neo attempts to charge a Killing Blow.

To defeat the Swordsman, Neo must evade his normal sword strike attempts and attack him from the side or behind. Use Special Attack moves to stun the Swordsman, and then press the Strike Button to begin a sword combo attack. When the Swordsman conjures doppelganger clones of himself, engage the doppelgangers one at a time until the true Swordsman is discovered.

SPECIAL ABILITIES
- BLADE CHARGE
- SWORD BLIND

STAGE APPEARANCE
Sword Training

DOBERMEN

These Exiles work for the Merovingian and populate his nightclubs. They are hulking, beastly looking brutes with werewolf-like features. Dobermen are capable of a variety of fighting moves. Dobermen are extremely aggressive and arrogant, not considering Neo to be a threat. And they stink, too!

When engaged in hand-to-hand combat, a Doberman attempts either of two types of modified Killing Blows, attempting to knock Neo off his feet.

Fighting a Doberman and the unique Doberman Boss is very much like taking on a squad of Agents. Although Dobermen are easier to knock down, they keep getting back up and coming back for more punishment. Use Focus frequently and attempt multi-opponent techniques, as Dobermen are trained to surround and attack from all sides. Use Weapon Strip moves to disarm them, concentrating efforts on bringing the battle down to a manageable level quickly.

SPECIAL ABILITIES
- HYPER EVADE
- RAGE

STAGE APPEARANCE
Redpill Rescue
The Frenchman
Downside Up

HONG KONG GUNRUNNERS

These simple training programs appear in a Hong Kong teahouse shootout stage that is reminiscent of two-fisted John Woo films like <u>Hard Boiled</u>. They only carry firearms, and are trained to return fire. Other than the Gunrunner Boss, who is programmed to lead Neo through the training exercise, regular Gunrunners will never retreat. During this training program, Neo's hand-to-hand abilities are negated. Therefore, his only available method of dispatching Gunrunners is to target enemies and fire. At extremely close range, with a firearm drawn, use Focus to kick an enemy into the air. Gunrunners are especially susceptible and weak against this attack.

SPECIAL ABILITIES
NONE

STAGE APPEARANCE
Weapon Training

INSECTOIDS

These bizarre, ant-man creatures are encountered in the surrealistic dungeons deep within the Merovingian's mansion. These inhuman monsters have the ability to disintegrate into a cloud of red dust, teleport to a new location, and reform. Insectoids use this ability to disappear momentarily and ambush Neo from behind. However, if a Killing Blow is performed while the Insectoid is mid-disintegration, it dies instantly.

Insectoids are also extremely weak against fire. Knock them into burning chandeliers or wield burning braziers against them using staff combos. Neo's only option is to use the environment to his advantage.

Insectoids have a spinning Aerial Killing Blow attack whereupon they leap into the air, spin for a second and then launch at Neo. Turn this attack against them by using Bullet Stop (Focus + Evade) to prevent this attack, and press the Fire Button to make the Insectoid disperse into a vulnerable red cloud.

SPECIAL ABILITIES
DISINTEGRATE
TELEPORT

STAGE APPEARANCE
Distorted Dimensions

JAPANESE ASSASSIN

Japanese Assassins encountered in the game are simple training programs designed to help Neo expand his sword fighting abilities to engage multiple opponents simultaneously. Their look and fighting style are reminiscent of classic Japanese samurai films, such as <u>Sword of Doom</u>. Unfortunately, the training program they exist in is suffering from a few system viruses. All Japanese Assassins will attack Neo when he approaches within a few feet.

Japanese Assassins attack mainly with their default weapon, usually a Katana. Use sword techniques to counter and strike Assassins, and attempt to learn Neo's melee skills.

SPECIAL ABILITIES
BLADE CHARGE

STAGE APPEARANCE
Winter Training

KUNG FU SOLDIER

Kung Fu Soldiers are competent martial arts students, studying the basics of hand-to-hand fighting techniques in a 70s style arch-villain's lair reminiscent of films like Enter the Dragon. They are the most basic training programs, designed to teach Neo how to fight hand-to-hand and how to use multi-opponent techniques. Defeat them easily by blocking their strikes, then grappling and counterstriking.

SPECIAL ABILITIES
NONE

STAGE APPEARANCE
Distorted Dimensions

POLICE

Police are the beat patrol officers who serve as rank and file minions of the System. Individual Police units are no match for rebels like Neo, Morpheus and Trinity. But they can become dangerous when equipped with Shotguns. Although they often appear in small groups, they act independently. Although they often shout warnings to each other, they are not capable of coordinating crossfire like more advanced tactical units. Police are extremely easy to take down, with either gunfire at long range or with hand-to-hand combos at close range.

SPECIAL ABILITIES
NONE

STAGE APPEARANCE
Ever Had a Dream, Neo?
They're Coming for You, Neo
He's Heading for the Street
Déjà Vu: "It's a Trap!"
He is the One

RIOT POLICE

Riot Police are SWAT-trained police officers with additional body armor, shields and heavy weaponry. Often encountered in small squads or with other types of Police and Security, Riot Police can be very dangerous enemies. They can carry a Riot Shield which turns a Riot Police officer into a moving cover position that other Police can take shelter behind. When in close range, a Riot Police officer holding a shield can use it to bash Neo to the ground. If a Riot Police officer is armed with a firearm, they constantly try to maintain a minimum distance of eighteen feet from the player.

Neo's incredible martial arts skills and grenades are the best ways to take out Riot Police. To make a Riot officer drop his shield instantly, attack him from behind.

SPECIAL ABILITIES
SHIELD BASH

STAGE APPEARANCE
Ever Had a Dream, Neo?
Lobby Shooting Spree
Rooftop Assault
Stuck in the Loop
The Security Guard
The Healer
Captains' Meeting
Captains' Rescue

PROGENY AND POTENTIALS

GUNS, LOTS OF GUNS

AND POTEN

WHAT IS THE MATRIX?

EXTRAS

UNLOCKING CHART

PROGRAMS

CONTROLLING PROGRAMS

PROGRAMS

UPGRADES

PATH OF THE ONE

15

SECURITY GUARD

Security Guards are very similar to Police, but their weapon capabilities are lower. Usually hired by private corporations to protect office and government buildings, Security Guards act independently during combat with a general concern for themselves and civilians. They shout warnings to others, but have no ability to coordinate crossfire like more advanced Riot Police and Soldiers.

When Security Guards identify a threat, such as Neo, they immediately draw their sidearm and seek cover. Security Guards can be taken out swiftly and easily, usually before they even have time to fumblingly take out their guns.

SPECIAL ABILITIES	STAGE APPEARANCE
NONE	Ever Had a Dream, Neo?
	They're Coming for You, Neo
	He's Heading for the Street
	Lobby Shooting Spree

SOLDIER

Soldiers are the top of the command chain in the System, coordinating local forces in raids and strikes against what they perceive to be the 'terrorist' threat of the rebels. Possessing greater health and strength, Soldiers also have the tactical knowledge to use various grenades and explosives as well as a Grenade Launcher.

Although Soldiers have some training in hand-to-hand, their abilities are restricted to the use of basic Strikes, Grapples and Evasion moves. Therefore, the best way to take out a Soldier is to move in close as quickly as possible and dazzle them with Neo's strong kung fu.

SPECIAL ABILITIES	STAGE APPEARANCE
NONE	Redpill Rescue
	Captains' Rescue

SWAT

By the time SWAT arrive on the scene, things have usually gone very wrong. SWAT units are called in only when it seems that normal police forces are ineffective against a criminal or that the criminal is sufficiently dangerous to pose a threat to police forces and bystanders. SWAT forces are the elite law enforcement units of the Matrix. Their ability to coordinate crossfire and use advanced weaponry makes them a force to be reckoned with. SWAT units are far better trained and equipped than lower ranking levels of police. Each SWAT team member carries fully automatic weapons and grenades.

In *Path of Neo*, SWAT units believe that they must stop what they consider to be a dangerous terrorist threat, possibly one that has already caused the deaths of their fellow police officers. SWAT units may also be under some kind of control from the Matrix itself. Agents are often the ones issuing orders to SWAT units. As a result, SWAT guys always attempt to kill the player on sight, by whatever means necessary.

Although they have some minor self-defense ability, the main strength of SWAT is their ability to use heavy weaponry. Approach within near range and strip their weapon to make them easily disposable.

SPECIAL ABILITIES	STAGE APPEARANCE
NONE	Ever Had a Dream, Neo?
	Déjà Vu: "It's a Trap!"
	Storming the Drain
	Lobby Shooting Spree
	Rooftop Assault
	Helicopter Rescue
	Redpill Rescue
	Captains' Rescue

VAMP

Vamps are thin, fast-living, stylishly dressed individuals. These slinky, leather-clad rogue programs are servants of the Merovingian. They prefer a life of excess and violence. Vamps are Exile programs, capable of employing advanced fighting moves such as running on walls and performing super jumps. Some Vamps can even walk on ceilings and shoot weapons while hanging upside down. Vamps always fight to the bitter end. They consider Neo to be merely another human and never run.

SPECIAL ABILITIES	STAGE APPEARANCE
BLADE CHARGE	Ever Had a Dream, Neo?
CEILING RUNNER	The Frenchman
HYPER EVADE	Downside Up

"GUNS. LOTS OF GUNS"

Although Neo gradually learns an array of hand-to-hand combat moves, there's no easier way to kill a foe than with a melee weapon or firearm. Firearms break down into three types: Semi-automatic, Automatic and Shotgun. Melee weapons are divided into types based on the different fighting style. When you have your choice of weapons hanging on the wall, what should you reach for? That's the burning question this chapter seeks to answer.

MELEE WEAPONS

Melee weapons can be used to fight in two ways: 1) they can either be used at close range to strike opponents, or 2) they can be thrown at close to medium range.

As in hand-to-hand combat, melee weapons can be used to link up multi-opponent combos. Striking at the same time an enemy strikes causes Neo to block.

To throw a melee weapon, press and hold the Target Lock button to lock on to an opponent. Use the Target Lock controls to switch targeted enemy. Press the Fire button to throw.

All melee weapons have a durability rating, and wear out after continued use. When a weapon reaches the end of its durability, it breaks and disappears from Neo's weapon cycle. Picking up a second weapon of the same type "strengthens" the durability of the weapon.

STICK

Sticks are short range melee weapons, which serve more as an enhancement to hand-to-hand combat. Neo spins to build momentum during strikes and combos, increasing the damage output.

WOOD STICK

A short length of wood. Provided as a "bonus weapon" by sneaking into the control room undetected during the "Kung Fu Training" stage.

DURABILITY — Medium

DURABILITY — Medium

SWORD

Swords are medium-length edged weapons that cut opponents. They are light and exceptionally easy to wield, allowing Neo to attack swiftly.

KATANA

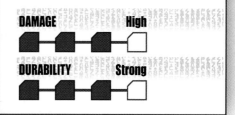

A steel Japanese sword. Typically carried by Japanese Assassins. Also found as collector's items in the Merovingian's Chateau.

DAMAGE — High

DURABILITY — Strong

CHINESE BROADSWORD

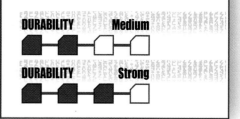

A Chinese army sword that is wider at the end, adding weight to the user's swing. A weapon collected by the Merovingian.

DURABILITY — Medium

DURABILITY — Strong

FORKED SWORD

A Manchurian-style blade that splits into three points at the end. Creates large wounds on opponents. Found hung on the walls of the Great Hall in the Merovingian's Chateau.

DURABILITY — Medium

DURABILITY — Strong

SWORD

A long, dual-edged sword carried by English knights of the Middle Ages. Has slightly better length than other swords, and its weight adds to its damaging power. Found in the Merovingian's lairs.

DURABILITY — High

DURABILITY — Strong

BOKKEN

A wooden practice sword. Breaks easily in the hands of rebels seeking to break the physics rules of the Matrix. Found in practice areas, such as the Dojo.

DAMAGE — Low

DURABILITY — Weak

STAFF

Neo can adapt any length of wooden or steel pole into a makeshift staff. Staves have excellent range as a melee weapon. Due to their swing and weight, controlling a staff is somewhat harder than with other melee weapons. Tilt the Movement Controls toward enemies when performing Strikes and Special Attacks. Avoid pressing the attack buttons too rapidly, or Neo could end up sailing past an evasive foe and find himself swatting at thin air.

BO STAFF

A four foot length of wood, typically used by martial arts students for practice. Can be found in the "Dojo Training" stage, sometimes carried by Morpheus, and also wielded by Smith copies. Swings very swiftly and allows for greater attack frequency.

DAMAGE — Medium

DURABILITY — Weak

STEEL GIRDER

A short pipe. Lasts a long time and knocks out opponents when thrown.

DAMAGE — High

DURABILITY — Very Strong

BURLY BRAWL STAFF

A sign post Neo rips out of the concrete during "The Burly Brawl" stage to use against Smith. A weapon with excellent damaging power and durability. Neo can sock plenty of Smiths out of the ballpark with this excellent choice of armament. The weight of this staff makes it a bit slower to swing.

DAMAGE — High

DURABILITY — Very Strong

CANDELABRA

A standing candle holder with a perpetually ignited top. Neo can use this weapon against the Insectoids who dwell in the Merovingian's "Distorted Dimensions", and can only be damaged by fire.

DAMAGE — Very High

DURABILITY — Medium

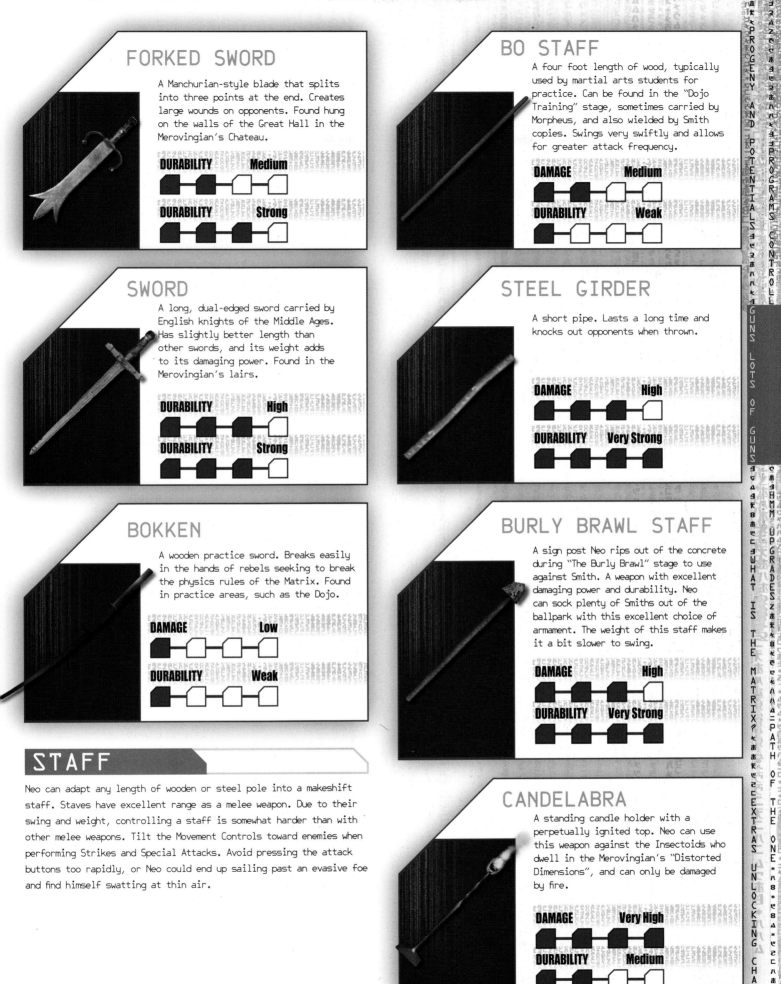

PROGENY AND POTENTIALS GUNS LOTS OF GUNS WHAT IS THE MATRIX? EXTRAS UNLOCKING CHARTS PROGRAMS CONTROLL UPGRADES PATH OF THE ONE

19

FLAGPOLE

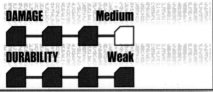

The long pole for hanging a flag, taken from the floor of the Senate House. It has a point at the top end, which though decorative is still quite sharp. Neo acquires this weapon to use against the Smith onslaught in the "Taking the Floor" stage.

DAMAGE   Medium

■—■—■—□

DURABILITY   Weak

■—■—■—■

MOP

A mop with a wooden handle, left on the stage of the theater in Chinatown. Either Neo or Seraph can use it to fight on the stage in front of the big screen. Although it swings quite easily, the Mop does little damage and does not last long.

DAMAGE   Medium

■—■—□—□

DURABILITY   Weak

■—□—□—□

BROOM

A broom with a wooden handle, left on the stage of the theater in Chinatown. Neo or Seraph can pick up this tool and use it to fight when their "battle of heart" crash-lands in Chinatown's local theater. The Broom does little damage, and does not last long in combat.

DAMAGE   Medium

■—■—□—□

DURABILITY   Weak

■—□—□—□

SPEAR

A Spanish style spear, usually found hanging on the wall in the collections of the Merovingian in his Chateau. The sharp point at the end make this an excellent weapon to use against foes. Unfortunately, Neo only gets to use it against the Witch boss, who is one of the strongest foes in the game!

DAMAGE   High

■—■—■—■

DURABILITY   Very Strong

■—■—■—□

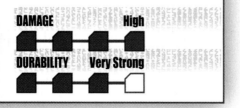

MORNINGSTAR

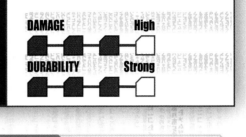

An extremely heavy steel pole with a spiked ball at the end. While this weapon deals great damage and bashes enemies right off their feet, its extreme weight makes it difficult to wield. Found among the weapon collections of the Merovingian, hanging in his game room.

DAMAGE   High

■—■—■—□

DURABILITY   Strong

■—■—■—□

AXE

Axes are small, light weapons for extremely short-range combat. Neo spins when using axes, to increase damage through the momentum. Axes are extremely accurate when thrown. All axes inflict light damage.

AXE GANG AXE

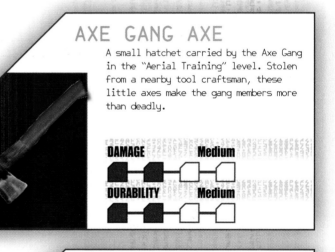

A small hatchet carried by the Axe Gang in the "Aerial Training" level. Stolen from a nearby tool craftsman, these little axes make the gang members more than deadly.

DAMAGE   Medium

■—■—□—□

DURABILITY   Medium

■—■—□—□

KAMA

A short, hand-held scythe-like weapon consisting of a foot-long handle and a curved blade. Crafted from steel, this weapon is extremely durable and carries well through the air when thrown.

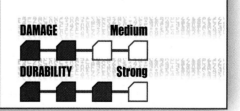

DAMAGE   Medium

■—■—□—□

DURABILITY   Strong

■—■—■—□

FIREARMS

SEMI-AUTOMATIC

Semi-automatic handguns discharge once each time the Fire button is pressed. If a handgun can be dual-wielded, the firing rate raises dramatically.

AUTOMATIC

Fully Automatic machineguns and rifles fire bullets continuously as long as the Fire button is held. SWAT, Soldiers, and Exiles often carry them.

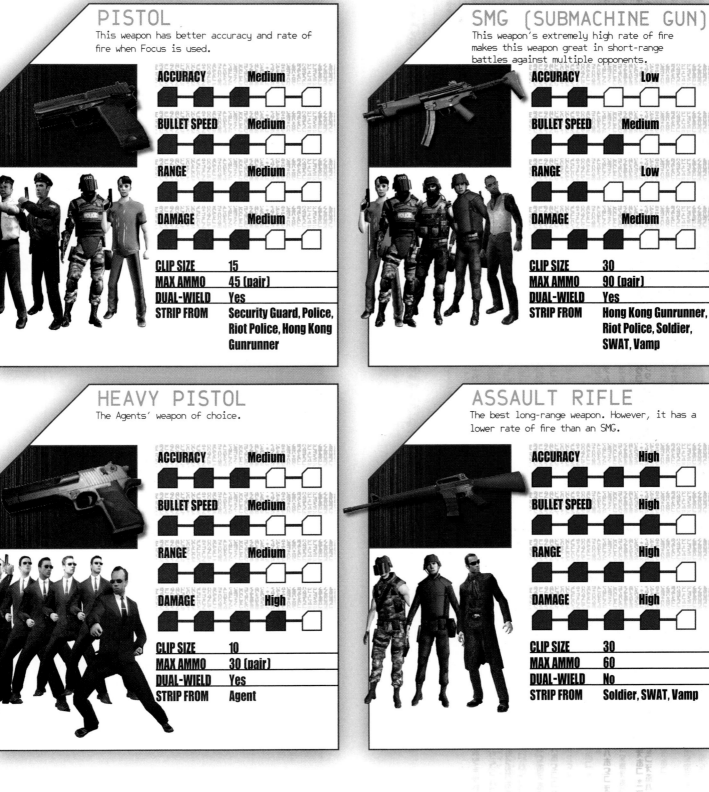

PISTOL

This weapon has better accuracy and rate of fire when Focus is used.

ACCURACY	Medium
BULLET SPEED	Medium
RANGE	Medium
DAMAGE	Medium

CLIP SIZE	15
MAX AMMO	45 (pair)
DUAL-WIELD	Yes
STRIP FROM	Security Guard, Police, Riot Police, Hong Kong Gunrunner

SMG (SUBMACHINE GUN)

This weapon's extremely high rate of fire makes this weapon great in short-range battles against multiple opponents.

ACCURACY	Low
BULLET SPEED	Medium
RANGE	Low
DAMAGE	Medium

CLIP SIZE	30
MAX AMMO	90 (pair)
DUAL-WIELD	Yes
STRIP FROM	Hong Kong Gunrunner, Riot Police, Soldier, SWAT, Vamp

HEAVY PISTOL

The Agents' weapon of choice.

ACCURACY	Medium
BULLET SPEED	Medium
RANGE	Medium
DAMAGE	High

CLIP SIZE	10
MAX AMMO	30 (pair)
DUAL-WIELD	Yes
STRIP FROM	Agent

ASSAULT RIFLE

The best long-range weapon. However, it has a lower rate of fire than an SMG.

ACCURACY	High
BULLET SPEED	High
RANGE	High
DAMAGE	High

CLIP SIZE	30
MAX AMMO	60
DUAL-WIELD	No
STRIP FROM	Soldier, SWAT, Vamp

SHOTGUN

Shotguns release a cone-shaped spread of shrapnel when fired, striking the target and all surrounding enemies in a narrow arc. They fire once each time the Fire button is pressed. Shotguns have an extremely low rate of fire, since they must be pumped or reloaded after each blast. Shotguns inflict more damage at close range.

SAWED-OFF SHOTGUN

These modified weapons have a short range and are extremely slow on the reload. However, they transfer massive damage to the target.

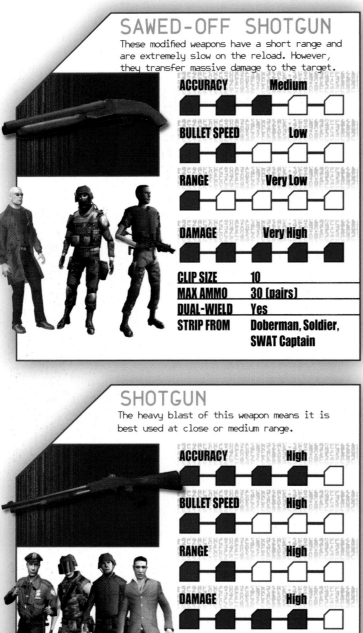

ACCURACY	Medium
BULLET SPEED	Low
RANGE	Very Low
DAMAGE	Very High

CLIP SIZE	10
MAX AMMO	30 (pairs)
DUAL-WIELD	Yes
STRIP FROM	Doberman, Soldier, SWAT Captain

SHOTGUN

The heavy blast of this weapon means it is best used at close or medium range.

ACCURACY	High
BULLET SPEED	High
RANGE	High
DAMAGE	High

CLIP SIZE	8
MAX AMMO	16
DUAL-WIELD	No
STRIP FROM	Police, Solder, SWAT, Vamp

GRENADES

Included in this category are all forms of detonation devices, whether the method is timed, by remote or on impact. Grenades should only be used or detonated when Neo is out of range. If caught in the blast, he may die instantly. If standing even at medium range, Neo could be slightly damaged and stunned by the force momentarily.

GRENADE LAUNCHER

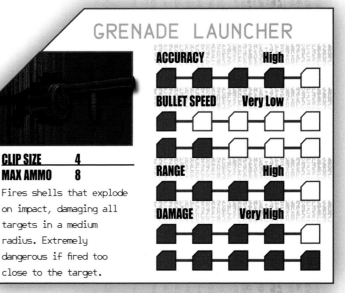

ACCURACY	High
BULLET SPEED	Very Low
RANGE	High
DAMAGE	Very High

CLIP SIZE	4
MAX AMMO	8

Fires shells that explode on impact, damaging all targets in a medium radius. Extremely dangerous if fired too close to the target.

FRAGMENTATION GRENADE

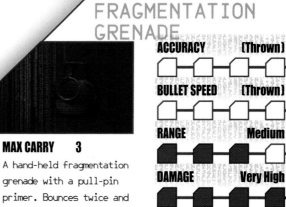

ACCURACY	(Thrown)
BULLET SPEED	(Thrown)
RANGE	Medium
DAMAGE	Very High

MAX CARRY	3

A hand-held fragmentation grenade with a pull-pin primer. Bounces twice and then explodes, damaging all enemies and objects within a medium blast radius.

Causes such extreme damage that most enemies are killed. Great to use against Agents, Riot Police, and large clusters of foes that should know better to spread out.

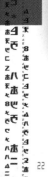

TEAR GAS GRENADE

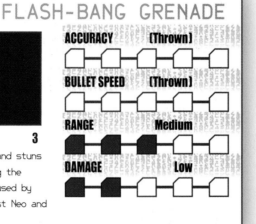

MAX CARRY   **3**

ACCURACY	(Thrown)
BULLET SPEED	(Thrown)
RANGE	Medium
DAMAGE	Low

A hand-thrown tear gas device that emits a choking cloud of smoke. All enemies caught within the cloud of smoke emitted by the device begin choking and wheezing, take small amounts of damage, and become mostly immobile. Some enemies with the "Gas Mask" ability are immune to the effects of tear gas.

FLASH-BANG GRENADE

MAX CARRY   **3**

ACCURACY	(Thrown)
BULLET SPEED	(Thrown)
RANGE	Medium
DAMAGE	Low

Causes blindness and stuns all enemies facing the blast. Sometimes used by Riot Police against Neo and the rebels.

DETONATION PACK

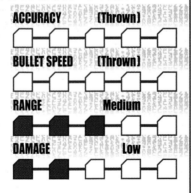

MAX CARRY   **3**

ACCURACY	(Thrown)
BULLET SPEED	(Thrown)
RANGE	Medium
DAMAGE	Low

A remotely-detonated explosive device used by SWAT and military forces to demolish obstacles and ambush rebels. When the Det Pack is selected in the weapon window, hold the Fire button to set the device near a gate, support column, or any location that you think SWAT are about to storm. After setting the Det Pack, the icon in the weapon window switches to the remote. Move a safe distance away and press the Fire button a second time to detonate the device. It destroys obstacles that prevent progress, and wipes out squads of even heavily armored foes.

"HMM, UPGRADES."

During <u>The Matrix: Path of Neo</u>, the One is able to acquire new abilities or improve combat skills in a special menu that appears between many stages. The One can be seen hovering in an abyss of code surrounded by four rings lined with abilities. This is called the Path of Neo screen.

Sometimes Neo acquires a skill merely by defeating certain enemies or by reaching a certain point in development. Other abilities are unlocked on the ring as possible upgrades. The icon on the ring is outlined rather than solid, meaning that the ability or upgrade is available, but has not been activated. Between most missions, the player can choose one skill or upgrade--signified by a yellow dot in the upper right corner of the Path of Neo screen. To activate a new skill or upgrade an existing skill, highlight the icon on the ring with the cursor and press the Select Button.

Upgrades can sometimes only be activated if another skill at a lesser level is already active. For example, Killing Blow must be active in order to activate Killing Blow Level 2.

Then there are Atman Principles, which are upgrades and abilities quite unlike all the others. Refer to the Atman Principles section farther back in this section to determine their function and duration.

SPECIAL ABILITIES

In line with Neo's progress in the films, he automatically learns Special Abilities. These abilities are awarded to Neo no matter what.

FOCUS
Focus Button

The Focus ability is learned by all rebels after they are disconnected from the Matrix and made aware of the flexibility of the "rules" of this simulation world. Press the Focus Button to slow down time, speed up Neo's movements, avoid bullets and enemy attacks, to improve attack power and damage, and to enable special movements such as Wall Run, Wall Jump, Bullet Dodge, Bullet Stop, etc.

Focus energy depletes while it is used. As long as energy remains in the Focus meter displayed onscreen below the health meter, Neo can remain in Focus mode. When Focus energy runs out, Neo automatically exits Focus mode. Therefore, this ability should be reserved for initiating Focus combo attacks or moves, and for fighting extremely powerful enemies such as Agents or Exiles. Neo automatically regenerates the bottom portion of the Focus meter. Focus can also be replenished by performing melee combat attacks against foes in real time, or by picking up a Focus Pack item.

Neo acquires the Focus ability during the training stage, "Kung Fu Training". As he progresses through stages and learns new abilities, Neo's Focus meter grows. A longer Focus meter allows Neo to remain in Focus mode longer.

4-HIT STRIKE COMBO

Strike Button x4

When Neo begins training, he starts with a simple 3 Hit Strike Combo. During the training stage, "Sword Training", Neo's default combo becomes extended by an additional move, allowing him to strike an opponent one additional time before reverting to a basic hand-to-hand stance.

OFF-WALL STRIKE

Wall Run or Wall Jump
Press Strike Button

Use Focus to perform a Wall Run or Wall Jump near an enemy. When Neo comes to a stop on the wall, press Strike to initiate an Off Wall Strike. Neo launches from an upright surface toward an enemy, delivering a powerful roundhouse kick. The enemy must be within just a few feet of the wall for this combo to work. This ability is learned during the training stage, "Dojo Training". Off Wall Strike is a growth ability that can be upgraded as Neo progresses through the game.

OFF WALL SUPER

Wall Run or Wall Jump
Press Special Attack Button

Use Focus to perform a Wall Run or Wall Jump near an enemy, then press the Special Attack Button at Neo's pause point to initiate an Off Wall Super. Neo leaps over an enemy's head, seizes them by the jaw and flips them across the room. This devastating move becomes available during the training stage, "Dojo Training".

AERIAL KILLING BLOW

Press Jump Button
Hold Focus Button and Special Attack Button
while midair to charge
Release to attack

Neo learns this skill after defeating Agent Smith during the "Subway Showdown" stage. While airborne after a jump or other move, hold the Focus

Button and the Special Attack Button to gather energy, as seen in the form of waves collecting around Neo. The release both Buttons to perform an Aerial Killing Blow on an enemy. Neo is vulnerable during the attack preparation, so be sure to use this only against single foes that are stunned or lying prone.

KILLING BLOW

Hold Focus Button
Hold Special Attack Button to charge
Release to attack

This move becomes available after the player defeats Ogami during the "Winter Training" stage and collects the scroll from the samurai's chest. Hold the Focus and Special Attack Buttons to gather energy, displayed as ripple waves surrounding Neo. Then release both Buttons to launch forward with a devastating punch. If Neo is equipped with a melee weapon, the Killing Blow changes depending on the type of weapon equipped. Neo is vulnerable to attack while charging the Killing Blow - it's best to unleash Killing Blows on enemies that have been stunned, to put them away quickly. Killing Blow can be improved to level 3.

DOUBLE JUMP

Press Jump Button
Press Jump Button again at peak

Neo gains this ability during the stage, "Rooftop Assault: 'Dodge This'." Perform a Focus Jump, then press Jump a second time at the highest point of Neo's initial leap to execute a mid-air flip, propelling Neo even higher.

FOCUS AERIAL THROW

Press Special Attack Button to stun
Hold Focus Button
Press Jump Button

After stunning an opponent, press and hold the Focus Button and press Jump to execute a Focus Aerial Throw. Neo lifts the enemy off their feet, flies straight up, and then tosses them to the ground. Neo slams the enemy into low ceilings for extra damage during this move. This Special Ability can be improved with additional upgrades gained later during the game. Neo learns this ability during the "Storming the Drain" stage.

BULLET DODGE

Hold Focus Button and Evade Button

Neo gains this ability during the stage, "Rooftop Assault: 'Dodge This'." When standing completely motionless and not in a hand-to-hand combat stance, hold the Focus Button and then hold the Evade Button to trigger Neo's trademark Bullet Dodge ability as seen in the original film. After becoming the target of an Agent, move far enough away that he draws his gun and begins firing. Another way to make him draw his weapon is to shoot at him from medium to long range. Initiate the Bullet Dodge move to avoid taking damage while a partner character moves in from the side and eliminates the distracted Agent.

WEAPON STRIP

Press Special Attack Button to stun
Press Fire Button

The Weapon Strip ability allows Neo to rip a gun from an enemy's hand after Grappling them. This skill becomes unlocked during the stage, "Déjà Vu: 'It's a Trap!'" When fighting an enemy that still has their weapon drawn, press Special Attack to stun them. Then press the Fire Button to disarm the opponent and flatten them. Weapon Strip can be improved several levels.

5-HIT COMBO

Strike Button x5

Expands Neo's default Strike combo to include 5 kicks, including a final Strike that makes an opponent airborne, setting them up for seize and slam moves or additional, aerial-triggered combos. Obtained automatically during the stage, "Déjà Vu: 'It's a Trap!'"

ANTIGRAVITY

Hold Focus Button
Press Jump

Neo learns this ability when needed while attempting to rescue the Security Guard during the "Redpill Rescue" stage. Essentially, Neo's inherent Focus Jump ability is improved so that Neo can soar higher than before. When combined with a Double Jump, Neo can leap from one level to the next without the use of stairs!

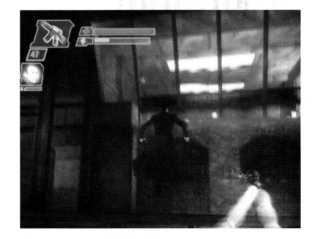

BULLET STOP

Hold Focus Button and Evade button

Acquired during the stage, "He is the One," this ability allows Neo to stop bullets fired at him in mid-air. Neo must be standing still and not in a hand-to-hand combat stance. Press and hold Focus as well as the Evade Button to stop bullets in their tracks. Continue holding both buttons to gather energy, and then press the Fire Button to fling the projectiles back at their owners!

6-HIT STRIKE COMBO

Strike Button x6

Rescue the martial arts instructor, Chuang Tzu, to acquire this ability during the "Redpill Rescue" stage. Neo become capable of an extremely graceful and powerful series of jump kicks and roundhouses, culminating in a devastating sideways flip kick that knocks an enemy at least twenty feet away.

MEGA PUNCH

Hold Focus Button
Hold Special Attack Button to charge
Release to attack

In a sense the ultimate Killing Blow, the Mega Punch is an ability that Neo learns automatically during the final series of boss fights against Smith. When Neo and Smith create a crater in the middle of the city street, Neo's Killing

Blow becomes replaced by this ability. Hold Focus and Special Attack to charge up this bad boy as usual, then release to strike. If the hit is successful, Neo smashes Smith's jaw in a special cinematic replicating the Mega Punch delivered during Matrix Revolutions. This is definitely worth seeing, so give it a shot!

CODE VISION

Press the Up Button of the digital pad

Allows the player to see the Matrix in code format, revealing the locations of hidden enemies, power-ups, items, doors and destructible environmental elements. Obtained after defeating Agents Jackson, Johnson and Thompson during the "Captains' Meeting" stage.

MASTER ABILITIES

Master Abilities start becoming available upon completion of the stage, "Déjà Vu: 'It's a Trap!'" Many of the Master Abilities are upgraded versions of Special Abilities. Certain Master Abilities can only be learned by rescuing potentials and rebel captains. Master Abilities are the hurdle; if Neo fails to learn certain Master Abilities, he becomes unable to learn some of the third level skills!

TORNADO THROW

Knock enemy off feet
Press Special Attack Button
Rotate Movement Control

This Master Ability becomes available for acquisition after clearing the stage, "Lobby Shooting Spree." This upgrades Neo's default ability to grab an enemy out of the air and slam them face-first into the ground. After performing a Mid-Air Grab, start rotating the Movement Control in circles immediately after slamming the person to the ground. Neo begins spinning

the victim in a circle, eventually releasing them into the surroundings. Any nearby enemies struck by the swinging opponent take severe damage and may be knocked several feet away. The target of this attack takes additional damage by colliding violently with the environment when flung.

AERIAL STRIKE LEVEL 2

Press Jump Button
Press Strike Button

This Master Ability becomes available for acquisition after completing the stage, "Subway Showdown." An upgraded version of one of Neo's default moves, this upgrade improves the damage done to a foe and increases the distance they get knocked backward. This move can be used to start, link or finish other combo moves. An Aerial Strike can be performed by either pressing Strike while airborne or by pressing Jump and then Strike.

OFF-WALL STRIKE LEVEL 2

Wall Run or Wall Jump
Press Strike Button

An improved version of Special Ability Off Wall Strike. After a Focus Wall Jump or Focus Wall Run, press Strike to leap from the surface with a powerful, two-fisted punch. This attack has greater range and damaging power at higher levels. Off Wall Strike Level 2 becomes available for acquisition after the stage, "Déjà Vu: "It's a Trap!"

OFF-WALL SUPER LEVEL 2

Wall Run or Wall Jump
Press Special Attack Button

An improved version of the Special Ability Off Wall Super. After leaping at or Wall Running along a wall, press the Special Attack Button to launch at a nearby enemy roughly ten feet away or less. Neo slams through the enemy with both fists. This move can also be modified; continue to hold Focus during the attack, and then press Target Lock and fire equipped weapons. In this method, Neo launches at an opponent, firing as he dives into the enemy's chest.

To illustrate an example, the modified Off Wall Super Level 2 replicates the move Neo performs as he leaps at Agent Smith during their confrontation in the subway station during the first *Matrix* film. This skill becomes available as an upgrade choice following the stage, "Lobby Shooting Spree."

AERIAL KILLING BLOW LEVEL 2

Press Jump Button
Hold Focus and Special Attack
Button while midair to charge
Release to attack

Rescue Morpheus and Trinity during the "Captains' Rescue" stage to make this Master Ability available on the second ring of the Path. Neo's Aerial Killing Blow improves in range and damaging power since Neo is now able to add several additional kicks to the maneuver.

KILLING BLOW LEVEL 2

Hold Focus Button
Hold Special Attack Button to
charge
Release to attack

An upgrade to the Killing Blow ability gained during the Winter Training stage. Only becomes available if Neo knows Killing Blow, upon clearing the stage "He is the One." After gathering energy, Neo now lashes out with a frenzied series of two-fisted punches and leaping kicks with both feet.

FOCUS AERIAL THROW LEVEL 2

Press Special Attack Button to stun
Hold Focus Button
Press Jump Button

Rescue dangerous martial artist Chuang Tzu from the clutches of the System during the **"Redpill Rescue"** stage to unlock this Master Ability. The Level 2 version is an expansion of the original move, allowing Neo to fly upward with an opponent as usual. Neo then places the enemy's face under his heel and slams his head into the ground. Damage output dramatically increases, especially when the opponent is slammed into a low ceiling. Also, Agents and Vamps can no longer escape or reverse the move.

WEAPON STRIP LEVEL 2

Press Special Attack Button to stun
Press Fire Button

Allows Neo to strip away an enemy's weapon when the foe is unaware of Neo's presence. Approach an unsuspecting enemy from behind and press the Special Attack to initiate the move, then press the Fire Button to take the target's weapon. Becomes available after the stage, "Déjà Vu: "It's a Trap!""

BULLET STOP

Hold Focus Button and Evade Button

Acquired during the stage, **"He is the One,"** this ability allows Neo to stop bullets fired at him in mid-air. Neo must be standing still and not in a hand-to-hand combat stance. Press and hold Focus as well as the Evade button to stop bullets in their tracks. Continue holding both buttons to gather energy, and then press the Fire button to fling the projectiles back at their owners!

AERIAL KILLING BLOW LEVEL 3

Press Jump Button
Hold Focus Button and Special Attack Button while midair to charge
Release to attack

Clear the **"Seraph's Apology"** stage. The highest upgrade of the Aerial Killing Blow becomes available for acquisition. This move allows Neo to target multiple enemies with the highest possible damage with an airborne attack, and also flings opponents extremely far across areas, severely hurting any other foes they happen to collide with. After leaping into the air, hold the Focus and Special Attack Buttons to charge up energy, then release to attack several foes. As Neo attacks the last target, rotate the Movement Control to finish with a 360 Clear Out.

PROGENY AND POTENTIALS • GUNS, LOTS OF GUNS • CONTROLLING PROGRAMS • WHAT IS THE MATRIX? • EXTRAS • UNLOCKING CHART • UPGRADES • PATH OF THE ONE

29

KILLING BLOW LEVEL 3

Hold Focus Button

Hold Special Attack Button to charge

Release to attack

Rescue Niobe during the "Captains' Rescue" stage to unlock the most powerful finishing move. At level 3, Neo can charge up enough energy to eliminate several enemies in quick succession. The move changes form depending on whether or not Neo is equipped with a melee weapon, and what type. As Neo attacks the last target, rotate the Movement Control to finish with a 360 Clear Out. When equipped with a Sign Pole during the "Burly Brawl" stage, try this move on Smith to perform Neo's famous "Around the Pole with 80 Kicks" combo!

FOCUS AERIAL THROW LEVEL 3

Press Special Attack Button to stun

Hold Focus Button

Press Jump Button

Rotate Movement Control

Clear the "Burly Brawl" stage. This Master Ability becomes available in Neo's third ring. Focus Aerial Throw Level 3 allows Neo to lift an enemy off the ground, slam them into a low ceiling, and then spin the enemy around and fling them into the environment in the same style as the Tornado Throw skill. Victims of this attack suffer environmental damage from hitting a low ceiling and from colliding with a wall or column after being thrown.

WEAPON STRIP LEVEL 3

Press Special Attack Button to stun

Press Fire Button

Save Captain Roland during the "Captains' Rescue" stage to unlock this skill upgrade. The highest level Weapon Strip allows Neo to grab an opponent and their weapon, shoot or strike another opponent in the vicinity, and then finish off the enemy holding the weapon.

FOCUS 360 CLEAR OUT

This Master Ability becomes available after rescuing the Librarian during the "Redpill Rescue" stage. Hold Focus, press Strike and Special Attack simultaneously, and then rotate the Movement Control in a circle. Neo draws up a small amount of energy and slams his fist into the ground, creating a ripple wave effect that knocks all enemies backward, possibly stunning them.

ATMAN PRINCIPLES

Atman Principles start becoming available after clearing the stage "Subway Showdown." Generally speaking, these are miscellaneous abilities that fall outside of permanent skills or damage upgrades. Unlike other abilities on the Path of Neo, most Atman Principles are temporary upgrades only. Read the description of each ability on the next page to determine the effect and how long it lasts.

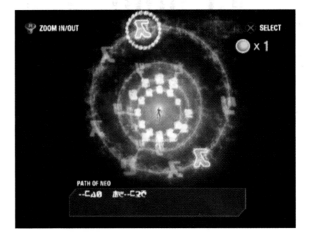

Many Atman Principles are encrypted in the Path of Neo screen. When the skill is highlighted with the cursor, only some garbled code appears. The code is decrypted only when chosen as an upgrade. Therefore, use this section to determine where the Atman Principles are located on the outer ring.

HEAL OTHERS

This is the first Atman Principle temporary skill upgrade to become available, after the player clears the "Subway Showdown" stage. On the outermost ring, Heal Others is located at 11 o'clock. Once chosen, this is a temporary ability available for one level only. Therefore, it is not a wise choice unless ally characters fight alongside Neo during the stage. The skill appears as an icon in Neo's weapon window. To use this ability, cycle through available weapons until the Heal Others icon is selected. Then hold the Fire

Button to activate the ability. Neo emits a short-range healing wave, restoring the health of all allies around him to 100 percent. Heal Others can be used three times, or until the next visit to the Path of Neo screen.

INSTANT REVIVE

Clear the stage, "He is the One." The Revive ability becomes available on the Atman Principles ring at roughly the 4 o'clock position. This is a temporary ability that lasts one stage only. When this ability is active, Neo automatically revives with full health if he is killed. Neo can only be revived once, and then no more.

REFLECT BULLETS

Neo enables this Atman Principle after rescuing Captain Ballard during the "Captains' Rescue" stage. The icon appears on the outer ring of the Path of Neo screen, at roughly the 5 o'clock position. The effect lasts only for the next stage. Reflect Bullets is like a weapon, and uses a slot in Neo's weapon cycle. To reflect bullets back at the enemies who fire them, cycle through the weapons in the weapon window until Reflect Bullets is displayed, and then press the Fire Button. When enabled, all bullets fired at Neo ricochet off him. The effect lasts one minute per use, and can be activated three times.

SPOON

For safely rescuing the Security Guard during the "Redpill Rescue" stage, the Spoon ability becomes available on the Atman Principle ring. To enable

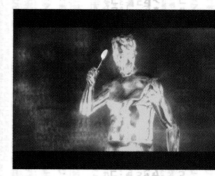

the Spoon upgrade, select the icon on the outer ring at the 8 o'clock position. This is a permanent upgrade, with a rather interesting animation video. The Spoon upgrade does not improve any of Neo's fighting abilities. Instead, acquiring this upgrade unlocks the Zion Archives stage in the Level Select screen.

JACKPOT

After rescuing The Healer during the "Redpill Rescue" stage, the Jackpot temporary ability becomes available. The icon appears on the outer ring of

the Path of Neo screen, in the 10 o'clock position. This Atman Principle takes the place of one of Neo's weapons and can be used by pressing the Fire Button. The effect raises Neo's Health, Focus, Health and Focus regeneration rates and damage output for all attacks. Jackpot lasts for three minutes, and can only be used once.

"WHAT IS THE MATRIX?"

"The Matrix is everywhere. It is all around us, even now, in this very room. You can see it when you look out your window, or when you turn on your television. You can feel it when you go to work, when you go to church, when you pay your taxes. It is the world that has been pulled over your eyes, to blind you from the truth: that you are a slave. Like everyone else, you were born into bondage, born into a prison that you cannot smell or taste or touch; a prison for your mind. Unfortunately no one can be told what the Matrix is. You have to see it for yourself."

- Morpheus

To conquer the Matrix requires a thorough knowledge of the rules upon which the system was founded. Also required is an open mind, and the belief that rules were meant to be broken. This chapter takes you inside the workings of The Matrix: Path of Neo, from its smallest nuances all the way to the Source.

CONTROLS

ACTION CONTROLS (DEFAULT SETTING)

CONTROL	PS2	XBOX	PC
MOVEMENT CONTROL	LEFT ANALOG STICK	LEFT THUMBSTICK	WSAD
CAMERA CONTROL	RIGHT ANALOG STICK	RIGHT THUMBSTICK	MOUSE
CYCLE INVENTORY	RIGHT/LEFT D-PAD	RIGHT/LEFT D-PAD	RIGHT/LEFT
HOLSTER/SWAP WEAPON	DOWN D-PAD	DOWN D-PAD	DOWN
CODE VISION*	UP D-PAD	UP D-PAD	UP
EVADE	SQUARE	X	CTRL
STRIKE	TRIANGLE	Y	MOUSE 1
SPECIAL ATTACK	CIRCLE	B	MOUSE 2
JUMP	X	A	SPACEBAR
FOCUS	L1	LEFT TRIGGER	SHIFT
ACTION/LINK-UP	L2	BLACK	TAB
FIRE GUN/THROW WEAPON	R1	RIGHT TRIGGER	MOUSE 1
DRAW GUN/TARGET LOCK	R2	CLICK RIGHT THUMBSTICK	F
CENTER CAMERA	R3	CLICK LEFT THUMBSTICK	
PAUSE MENU	START	START	ESC
WEAPON STRIP	NA	NA	Q
THROW MELEE WEAPON	NA	NA	T

*Ability is unlocked with upgrade.

MENU CONTROLS (DEFAULT SETTING)

CONTROL	PS2	XBOX	PC
MOVE CURSOR	LEFT ANALOG STICK	LEFT THUMBSTICK	ARROW KEYS
SELECT	X	A	ENTER
CANCEL	TRIANGLE	Y	BACKSPACE
NEXT SCREEN	R1	RIGHT TRIGGER	
PREVIOUS SCREEN	L1	LEFT TRIGGER	
SKIP SCENE	X	A	ENTER*

*Requires previous viewing.

MENUS

OPTIONS MENU

Two Option menus are available in the game. The main Option menu is available on the title screen. The other is a modified version that can be selected from the Pause Menu while playing a stage.

Audio

Allows you to adjust the balance of background music to sound effects to voice dialog.

Video

The options in this menu affect the graphic presentation of the game. The brightness can be adjusted to suit your monitor. The Aspect Ratio allows you to switch between normal screen (4:3) and wide-screen (16:9). Fine adjustments can be made to the lighting detail in levels to make it easier to see in shadows, although other areas may become slightly washed out.

Languages

Turn the game dialog and movie montage subtitles on or off.

Controller Options

Allows the player to adjust certain control functions. Target Lock can be made into a toggle rather than a hold function. In toggle mode, press the Target Lock button once to activate the targeting crosshairs, and press it again to exit Target Lock. If Neo is equipped with firearms, he will not holster the weapons until Target Lock is deactivated.

Invert Y and Invert X allows you to change how the Camera Controls operate. The Y-axis is the up and down motion of the camera, and the X-axis controls side to side angling.

Controller Configuration

The default configuration listed above is known as configuration "Alpha". On this screen, tile the Movement Control left or right to cycle through other available button configurations. Configuration Beta changes the function of all face buttons, and Gamma switches only the Fire and Evade buttons.

NEW GAME

Select "Start" from the title screen to begin a new game. Choose an empty file slot in which to record data between stages. Or, choose an old save game to overwrite. The game automatically saves your progress after each stage is completed. In the PlayStation2 version, a memory card must be inserted into slot 1 for the auto-save function to work.

THE AUTO-SAVE ICON

The auto-save icon indicates that the game is in the process of recording data and your progress to the hard drive or memory card of your gaming system. Avoid resetting or turning off the game until the auto-save icon disappears from the screen. The game typically auto-saves the game after each stage, or at the start of each new stage.

LOAD GAME

If save data exists on your system or on a memory card inserted into the console, choose Load Game to proceed to the Game Menu. The first option allows you to quickly jump right back in where the action left off. The last option takes you back to the title screen.

Level Select

The Level Select option enables the replaying of previously visited stages. However, note that going back to a previous level overwrites current progress, and levels higher than the one chosen become unavailable again. After the entire game is cleared, all levels become

permanently unlocked in the Level Select screen, allowing you to replay any level without accidentally locking higher levels.

Whenever a level is replayed, Neo's abilities return to their settings at the start of the level. Backtracking causes Neo to lose upgrades and skills that may have been obtained by completing higher levels or clearing the game.

Extras

Contains several sub-screens chock full of bonuses and special features. All Extras are unlocked by completing certain stages, or by obtaining special Briefcase items hidden in out of the way locations. Once you have obtained a Briefcase or cleared a stage, allow the game to auto-save. Next time you boot up The Matrix: Path of Neo, check the Extras Menu to see what's new.

To learn how to unlock secrets, refer to the bonus sections sprinkled throughout the **Path of the One** chapter, and also refer to the handy **Extras Unlocking Chart** at the back of the book.

Movies

Movie montages cultivated from the three Matrix films and The Animatrix, created specifically for **The Matrix: Path of Neo**. Movies become unlocked in the Extras Menu after they are seen in the game.

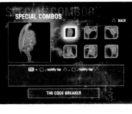

Special Combos

Hand-to-hand and melee combat are made easier by unlocking these bonus combos in the Extras Menu. Although most Special Combos look like a crazy hodge-podge of button dancing, they can easily be triggered during the course of combat. Just try to keep the Special Combo button inputs in mind, and realize when you are just one or two button presses away from finishing off the enemy with one of these moves.

Media Viewer

The Media Viewer in the Extras Menu contains several pages of still artwork pieces, which were drawn up and used in the process of creating The Matrix: Path of Neo. Unlock the pages by fulfilling certain criteria during the stages of the game.

Cheats

Completing the game at least once entitles you to an easier ride next time. Cheats become unlocked by clearing the game on certain difficulty levels.

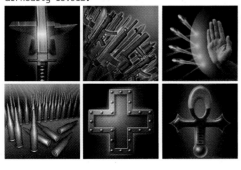

The Making Of...

A screen containing special video clips that document the making of the game. Content includes storyboard to finished cinematic comparisons, and montage clips showing off all of Neo's killer moves.

PAUSE MENU

While controlling Neo, press the Pause button to bring up the Pause Menu. The Matrix shows its code, and several options become available. Choose the first option to resume play, and select the last option to quit playing and exit to the title screen.

Objectives

Displays a screen of stage objectives and bonus objectives. As objectives are achieved, they become darkened in the Objective screen. "Objectives Updated" messages appear during game play, indicating that either new objectives have been added to the list or old objectives have been fulfilled.

Options

A curtailed version of the main Options Menu available on the title screen. This version allows for the tweaking of sound levels, lighting adjustments, and screen changes.

Controls

Change the control scheme and game play options mid-stage to make the situation more comfortable for your style of play.

Retry

Restart the current level from the last checkpoint. Checkpoints are like saving way stations along the path of the One. Checkpoints are not recorded to the hard drive or memory card. Instead, checkpoints are like reminders to the game that you have surpassed a certain point in the stage. If you reset your console or exit a stage, the level must be replayed from the beginning.

THE PATH OF NEO SCREEN

Between certain stages, the game exits to a special screen that illustrates Neo's developing abilities and allows the player to choose new upgrades when available. The One can be seen floating in a void between four skill rings. Each ring is lined with Neo's Special Abilities and Master Abilities. Use the Movement Control to highlight abilities, and press the Select button to read skill descriptions and choose them. Press the Up Button or Down Button on the digital pad or keyboard to move up one ring or down one ring. After an ability is selected (if necessary), press the Continue button to proceed to the next stage.

Special Abilities are generally found on the lower levels of the rings, as most of them are obtained automatically during the early stages of the game. Master Abilities and the powerful Atman Principles are found on the upper levels. Many of these selectable skills are upgrades of lower level skills, improving Neo's damage output.

When a gold icon is displayed in the upper right corner of the Path of Neo screen, a skill upgrade must be chosen before the player can move on. Upgrades and new abilities become available to choose after clearing certain stages or by fulfilling certain criteria in the game.

The Path of Neo

Look for "Path of Neo" sections throughout the walkthrough chapter. These sections detail what upgrade choices become available on this screen, and when.

DIFFICULTY SETTING

The difficulty setting is not chosen from a menu when starting the game. Instead, the player must prove his or her worthiness to become the One by surviving an opening challenge stage. Neo finds himself in a dreamlike version of the Government Building Lobby. Waves of enemies continuously enter the room. Defeat as many foes as possible to unlock higher difficulty settings.

If the player runs out of health and Neo dies, the game determines what difficulty settings to offer based on how far the player got in the challenge stage. The player then chooses from available difficulty settings to proceed.

> Your skill allows you to walk the Path of the One.
>
> Accept this difficulty setting?
>
> The One (Hard)
> Master (Normal)
> Disciple (Easy)
> Retry challenge.
>
> Press × to select.

DISCIPLE

This is the easiest setting. This difficulty setting is tuned for a more mainstream audience, with little or no experience in game playing. Disciple is no walk in the park. The latter stages should still prove arduous. This difficulty should provide a good challenge for casual gamers ages 13 and up. This difficulty is unlocked by merely starting the first level.

MASTER

This is the normal game play setting, finely tuned and balanced to capture the true Matrix experience. Seasoned video game players should find this mode challenging. Enemies employ blocks and counter moves more frequently than in Disciple mode. Greater numbers of enemies appear in certain stages. This difficulty setting is unlocked by eliminating the first wave of enemies in the opening challenge stage.

THE ONE

This difficulty setting provides a challenge to gamers out to 'prove' something to themselves or others. In addition to blocks and counter moves, enemies' firing accuracy is sharply improved. The only hope of avoiding bullets lies in using Focus, almost constantly. Greater numbers of enemies appear in certain stages, even more so than in Master mode. The One difficulty setting becomes available if the player can defeat all opponents in the opening challenge stage, including Agent Smith.

HUD (HEADS UP DISPLAY)

1. WEAPON WINDOW: Shows the weapon that Neo is currently equipping. If the weapon is a firearm, Neo keeps the gun(s) holstered until the Target Lock button is pressed. When the arrows appear to either side, the player can cycle through available weapons by pressing the Left or Right buttons. Neo can carry up to three firearms or melee weapons at a time.

2. AMMO INDICATOR: Displays the total amount of ammunition remaining for the equipped firearm. If the equipped item is a melee weapon, the window flashes to indicate that the durability of the weapon is reduced and that it is about to break.

3. ALLY HEALTH: If Neo is fighting with a partner such as Trinity, Morpheus, or another rebel fighter, their health is displayed onscreen. Monitor ally health closely; sometimes your own life depends on theirs.

4. SWITCH WEAPON: Press the Down button to swap the currently displayed weapon for one that is lying on the ground.

5. HEALTH: Displays the current amount of Neo's health remaining. When reduced to zero, Neo dies and the game ends. The health bar becomes longer as Neo progresses through the game and becomes more impervious to damage.

6. FOCUS: Indicates the amount of Focus energy remaining. Focus energy is Neo's "magic power", allowing him to bend the rules of the Matrix.

7. ENEMY HEALTH: Displays the remaining health of prominent enemies in the vicinity, known as "bosses". When these foes are taken down, the remaining enemies suffer.

ITEMS

Valuable pickups lying in the environment glow to catch the player's eye. Obtain these items by walking over them. Items can be found located in the environment. Defeated or disarmed opponents may drop items.

HEALTH PACKS

Replenish Neo's health. Most Health Packs restore up to 75% of Neo's Health meter when extended to its fullest. Health packs come in various forms, depending on the theme of the environment.

FOCUS PACKS

Recharge Neo's Focus energy, allowing him to see just how far the rabbit hole goes.

Firearm

Guns are highlighted with a purple aura. Neo can carry up to three firearms. If Neo has space remaining in his inventory, he can pick up a weapon. If Neo already possesses the weapon type, his ammo count grows when he picks up additional guns.

Melee Weapon

Melee Weapons such as swords or staves are highlighted with a green aura. Neo can tote three melee weapons at once. If Neo already has the weapon type he is trying to pick up, the weapon's durability is strengthened back to full.

Briefcase

A bonus item hidden in obscure places in stages. Sometimes Briefcases do not appear until certain criteria are fulfilled. These items unlock bonus features in the Extras menu.

BASIC ACTIONS

MOVEMENT

Navigate through the environment using the Movement Control. Depending on the gaming system, the Movement Control can be used to determine the rate of speed. Move the Movement Control only slightly and Neo walks. Move the control all the way and Neo runs at full speed.

When Neo runs, he makes noise that can be heard by surrounding enemies. If you find an enemy's back turned, move up slowly behind them and press the Special Attack button to initiate a Silent Takedown, as described in the Hand-to-Hand Combat section below.

Hold the Focus button while running to move more quickly than usual. This is helpful in avoiding punches, kicks, bullets and flying debris.

DOORS AND BUTTONS

Press the action button when facing a door to open it. Doors can only be opened when the Action button icon appears onscreen. If Neo is standing still, he opens the door slowly and quietly. If Neo is running toward the door when the Action Button is pressed, he slams through the door violently. Slamming through a door can be advantageous when dangerous enemies are in hot pursuit. However, the action causes loud noise that may alert enemies on the other side of the door...

Use the Action Button to activate buttons and levers on control panels for devices found in certain stages. If you approach a control panel and the Action Button icon appears onscreen, press the button to activate the device.

JUMPING

Press the Jump button while running to leap over gaps and jump over environmental objects. As Neo progresses in the game, he unlocks new abilities that increase the height to which he can jump. He also gains the ability to Double-Jump, giving him an extra boost by flipping in mid-air. Learn to gauge how high and how far Neo can jump, so when the time comes, you can make the jump, instead of falling to the pavement below.

Focus can be used to raise and elongate Neo's jump arc. A Focus Jump allows Neo to clear larger gaps and chasms, and also allows him to reach higher levels more easily.

EVADE

Press the Evade button to avoid enemy attacks during combat. If Evade is pressed when Neo stands perfectly still, he performs a back flip. The direction Neo moves to avoid attack can be controlled using the Movement Control. By propelling Neo to the side of an enemy or over an enemy's head during an Evade, you can reposition him to a more advantageous position flanking the enemy. Thus, Evade moves can be used not only to avoid damage, but also to take the enemy by surprise!

STUN

Stun is a 'condition' that afflicts Neo sometimes when an enemy is blocking too many attacks, or when Neo suffers damage, or when a hand-to-hand combat strike misses the mark. Some enemies employ attacks specifically designed to inflict stun.

Stun occurs at two levels. Mild stun is displayed by a green code indicator around Neo's head. The controller becomes less responsive. In this state, Neo is vulnerable to enemy combo attacks and Killing Blows.

If Neo begins to stagger or waver back and forth as if about to pass out, this indicates a more advanced state of stun. Typically, Neo suffers this state after being struck by advanced enemy attacks and Killing Blows. The controls become completely unresponsive, and Neo is vulnerable to any attack. Rapidly tap the Evade button to break free of advanced stun, before Neo takes additional damage.

Enemies suffer from stun the same as Neo. By tilting the Movement Control toward an enemy and pressing Evade, Neo might be able to do an over-the-head evade. While flipping through the air over an enemy, Neo plants a hand on their head, possibly stunning them. Some advanced enemies can counter this move, throwing Neo to the ground.

LINK-UP

When near a flat wall, press the Action button to engage in a Link-Up with the surface. Neo presses his back against the wall. In this position, you can use the Movement Control to slide in either direction along the wall.

At a corner, tilt the Movement Control toward the area around the turn to make Neo lean out for a better look. This is an excellent way to get a better view of an area without being spotted.

While Linked-Up to a wall near a corner, tilt the Movement Control out and press Jump to dive out into the open. If there is another corner just across the passage, Neo automatically links up to it.

If Neo is equipped with a firearm, press the Target Lock button and lean out from the corner to target an enemy. Press the Fire Button to step out and fire. Release the Fire Button to retreat back around the corner. While firing, press the Jump Button to leap out and attack.

CLIMBING

Move toward ladders and low objects to start climbing. Neo automatically steps over small, waist-high obstacles. To get around larger obstacles or to reach higher ledges, jump toward the surface and Neo will grab hold of the edge. At this point, tilt the Movement Control up to climb onto the surface, or press the Jump Button to drop to the level below.

CAMERA CONTROL

If ever you lose sight of enemies or cannot see who is firing, use the camera controls to help. Press the Camera Reset button to center the camera behind Neo. This is an important function, so be sure to map it to a memorable button. To adjust the looking angle higher or lower, for instance to see over an edge or try to spot a platform above, tilt the Camera Control to change the view.

ADDITIONAL ACTIONS

As the player progresses in the game, Neo's abilities expand and improve. He also learns new abilities, such as Code Vision and Antigravity. Abilities learned or made available during the course of the game are detailed in the chapter titled "Hmm, Upgrades."

FOCUS

Focus is like Neo's "magic power". By activating Focus, Neo can move faster, strike harder, and perform moves and actions that are impossible without Focus. When a hand-to-hand combo is performed without Focus, it is pretty standard martial arts stuff. But when Focus is applied to the same combo, Neo's moves become broader, crazier, and more dangerous.

Press and hold the Focus button to activate Focus. This ability can only remain active as long as Neo has Focus energy remaining. After various events in the course of the game, Neo's Focus meter extends. The longer the meter, the more time Neo can spend in Focus and the more damage he can do.

Focus improves firearm aiming and thereby causes greater damage to enemies with each shot. Neo's Focus ability also makes it easier to evade bullets and enemy punches or kicks, since in slow motion these attacks can be seen in motion a full second before they land.

The bottom twenty-five percent of the full Focus meter recharges automatically after the Focus button is released. To regain more Focus, attack enemies with hand-to-hand or melee weapon combos in real time. Focus Packs can also be picked up to refill the meter.

FOCUS ACTIONS

As mentioned in the previous section, certain actions only become available when Focus is used.

Wall Run

While running directly toward a wall or flat vertical surface, press and hold the Focus Button to initiate a Wall Run. Neo runs directly up the wall. This ability can be used to quickly surmount small ledges.

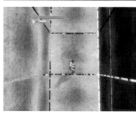

If the wall is very high, or extends up to a ceiling, Neo runs up the wall to a certain point and then crouches. If you continue to hold the Focus Button and press Jump in this moment, a Wall Jump can be executed.

Wall Jump

Hold the Focus Button and jump toward a wall. When Neo touches the wall, he connects to it and coils up as if ready to pounce. Press Jump again when Neo curls up to initiate a Wall Jump. Neo leaps off the wall in the direction indicated by the Movement Control. This action allows Neo to leap higher, especially before the Double-Jump ability is obtained.

Neo can Wall Jump from one surface to another, continually rising higher as long as Focus energy is available. In the early stages of the game or in any emergency, this action can be used to reach higher levels and platforms. Wall Jumps performed to reach higher platforms are more successful in a corner, where two walls meet.

HAND-TO-HAND COMBAT

The main form of combat in the game, hand-to-hand combat is always available to the player, even if weapons are not. In the first few stages of the game, Neo is "plugged in" to the Matrix and has no super powers or combat abilities. The most he can do is shove a Policeman or Security Guard backwards when the Strike Button is pressed. After Neo takes the red pill and becomes a child of Zion, he undergoes extensive combat training. Hand-to-hand Combat or martial arts is part of that training.

As the player progresses in the game, Neo gains new abilities and his martial arts skills expand. With more moves at the player's disposal, the game becomes easier.

STRIKE

Press the Strike Button to punch or kick an enemy. Strikes are the building blocks of all combos and advanced attacks. Use strikes to cut through an enemy's defenses. Once a strike is successful, follow up with a Special Attack and then try to trigger a combo.

Block attacks by pressing the Strike Button when an enemy attempts a hand-to-hand attack. Similarly, enemies can block Neo's attack in the same way.

At the start of his combat training, Neo knows only a very basic striking pattern. Pressing the Strike button three times in a row causes Neo to attempt three attacks before resettling in a hand-to-hand combat stance. This limited combo allows enemies more opportunities to attack between Neo's combos without being blocked. As Neo progresses in the game, this basic strike combo expands to four Strikes, then five, then six. The more strikes Neo can perform in a row, the more likely he is to cut through an enemy's defense and land a damaging punch or kick.

SPECIAL ATTACK

Press the Special Attack Button to attempt to grapple with an opponent. A Special Attack is more likely to be successful when an enemy is already off-balance following a successful Strike.

You can use Special Attacks to stun and throw opponents, but the main function of Special Attack is to open up opponents to attack combos. After a Special Attack, button icons appear onscreen. Pressing these buttons while they remain onscreen triggers a "combination" or "combo" attack. Combos put the "special" in Special Attack.

When a combo is triggered, Neo begins performing a rapid-fire series of attacks that resembles a graceful ballet of death. Having been rendered defenseless by the Special Attack, the enemy is helpless against the move and gets the throttling of a lifetime. Neo typically finishes most combos by knocking an opponent across the room like a sack of potatoes. However, combos can be extended with certain well-timed button presses, allowing Neo to continuously bash even boss enemies from full health to fully dead in a matter of seconds. Just watch the screen and press the appropriate button when its icon appears.

Press and hold the Focus button during a Special Attack to make additional, Focus-based combos available. When Focus is added to the mix, Neo's action style takes on an entirely cinematic quality rivaling any Hong Kong martial arts film. However, if Focus energy runs out during a combo attack, the assault cannot be extended with additional button presses.

Most enemies are capable of a Special Attack as well. In fact, an enemy can use a Special Attack to counter Neo's Special Attack--and vice versa. If an enemy successfully performs a Special Attack on Neo, they will seize him and perform an unstoppable series of attacks. Agents, for instance, like to bend Neo over their knee and commence pounding rapidly on his chest in what is known as a Fist Bouquet. Neo is more susceptible to enemy Special Attacks when he is suffering from any level of stun.

THROWS

After successfully performing a Special Attack on an enemy, tilt the Movement Control forward of Neo's direction of facing to throw the opponent across the room. Throwing an enemy behind Neo is also possible; just tilt the Movement Control away from the direction Neo faces. Throws are best to use when you're surrounded and want to clear the area, when you  can throw one enemy into another, or when you can throw an enemy over a ledge or into a dangerous object, like an electrified pool of water.

AERIAL ATTACKS

After a couple of upgrades, Neo becomes able to attack foes from just about every angle. One extremely strategic angle to attack from is directly overhead.

Whenever Neo is airborne, or just after a jump, hold the Focus Button and press the Strike Button to execute a midair reversal and kick. Neo flies toward an enemy and boots them right under the chin.

Aerial attacks can also be performed during or just after a Wall Run or Wall Jump. When Neo comes to a stopping position, continue to hold Focus and press the Strike or Special Attack Buttons. If an enemy is within a given distance across from Neo's position on the wall, he flies out and attacks the foe in a manner similar to the move he used against Smith in the final battle of The Matrix Revolutions.

WEAPON STRIP

When the Weapon Strip skill becomes available, Neo can disarm an opponent by pressing the Special Attack Button and then the Fire Button. In the PC version, Weapon Strip has its own button. An enemy can only be disarmed when they have their gun or melee weapon in hand.

If an opponent is armed with a gun, they may holster their weapon when Neo moves in close range. This makes a Weapon Strip harder to achieve. The best way to make an enemy draw their gun is to shoot at them while moving within close range.

As Neo's Weapon Strip ability improves, he becomes able to take an opponent's weapon and attack them with it. At mastery level, Neo can seize an opponent, use the weapon they hold against other foes in the vicinity, and then turn it on the wielder. If too many bullets are flying for your liking, use Weapon Strip attacks to level the playing field.

KILLING BLOW

Learned in an early training stage, the Killing Blow is the ultimate finishing move in Neo's arsenal. To perform a Killing Blow, hold the Focus Button and the Special Attack Buttons to charge up the attack. Waves of energy begin gathering to Neo, and he drops down into a pouncing stance. Release the Special Attack button to commence the Killing  Blow. Based on the level of skill upgrade achieved, the Killing Blow could take the form of an extremely powerful punch, or Neo could string together a series of wicked looking attacks.

Charging up the Killing Blow leaves Neo vulnerable to attack. Therefore, choose the opportune moment wisely. Attempt a Killing Blow only if the enemy is showing signs of stun, or if they have been knocked down and are a little slow to get up.

Enemies can also perform Killing Blows. If an enemy crouches and seems to be gathering tension, it means they are charging a Killing Blow and preparing to unleash. Strike the opponent to cancel their Killing Blow, or use Evade to get out of range.

MID-AIR GRAB

After knocking an opponent off their feet, quickly press the Special Attack button. Neo grabs the flying enemy by their legs and slams them into the ground. A few upgrades

later, Neo becomes capable of the Tornado Throw. After slamming the enemy face-first into the asphalt, he can then spin the enemy around and fling them into the environment.

MULTI-OPPONENT COMBAT

When Neo is facing an opponent in a hand-to-hand combat stance, all of his Strikes and Special Attacks will be directed toward that one enemy. The target that Neo is facing during hand-to-hand combat is said to be "Online". However, several "Offline" opponents may also surround Neo. Without hesitation, they begin to sucker punch Neo from his side or rear.

Opponents surrounding Neo in a hand-to-hand fight can be controlled and utilized with "Multi-Opponent Combat" techniques. For instance, move the Movement Control toward an Offline opponent and press the Strike button to attack the enemy. Neo doesn't even look at the foe as he attacks them, catching them totally off-guard.

Multi-Opponent Special Attacks can also be engaged, allowing Neo to perform some of the most eye-catching combos in the game. At the exact moment you perform a Special Attack on one foe, tilt the Movement Control toward another enemy and press Special Attack again. There should be little hesitation between the two times Special Attack is pressed. If done correctly, Neo should knock both opponents off their feet and then do something nasty to them. If button timing is unsuccessful, Neo simply throws one foe into the other.

AIR WALK

When faced with an army of opponents, such as a large group of Smith copies, it is possible to get out of the center of things with Air Walk. After jumping and landing on an enemy's head, use the Movement Control to guide Neo toward other enemies. If the next enemy is nearby, Neo jumps from one head to the other, as seen in The Burly Brawl from The Matrix Reloaded.

MELEE WEAPONS

Neo can equip various melee weapons to improve his damaging power and fighting speed. Such weapons include swords, staves, spears, hatchets, sticks, pipes, and more. Melee combat is carried out much the same as hand-to-hand combat: Strikes can be used to block strikes or attack, and Special Attacks can be used to trigger powerful combo moves. Focus employed with a melee weapon is a beautiful thing.

When Neo equips a melee weapon, his fighting style changes dramatically. The manner in which Neo moves and strikes depends on the type of melee weapon equipped. Melee weapons are categorized by type in the chapter titled "Guns. Lots of Guns."

Killing Blows, Weapon Strips and Aerial Attacks can still be employed when melee weapons are equipped, with extremely dramatic results. To switch back to hand-to-hand combat, press the Down Button on the digital pad or keyboard. After Neo puts the weapon away, press the Left or Right Buttons to equip the weapon again.

THROWING MELEE WEAPONS

Melee weapons can be thrown at opponents standing at close to medium range. First, improve accuracy and target the opponent by holding the Target Lock Button. Then press and hold the Fire Button to throw the weapon at the foe. Throwing melee weapons is a great way to knock an opponent off their feet, rendering them susceptible to a Killing Blow or Special Attack.

WEAPON DURABILITY

Some things about the Matrix were programmed all *too* well. Melee weapons break after extended use. The more a staff or sword is used, the greater its degradation. Eventually, melee weapons break and disappear from Neo's hands.

It is possible to stack melee weapons to increase their durability. If a melee weapon in hand is growing weak, pick up another one exactly like it to extend the weapon's durability.

FIREARMS COMBAT

Firearms combat is quite different than fighting with martial arts - it's really a combat system all its own. After picking up a firearm, either one dropped by an enemy or taken from him directly with Weapon Strip, hold the Target Lock button to draw the firearm and press the Fire Button to shoot. Firearms allow you to take out enemies at range, and also allow you to safely close the distance between enemies so you can take them out with martial arts moves.

Target Lock automatically prioritizes enemies in front of Neo and generally to the center of his field of vision. You can switch targets by thumbing the camera controls in the direction of the desired target (for the PS2 and Xbox versions, the right control stick). To target enemies 180 degrees behind you, quickly tip the Target Lock control directly back. Also, when he's in the air, Neo can target enemies in all directions.

When in Target Lock, Neo's normal movement switches to strafing movement, allowing you to keep your targets centered in your field of vision. Also, Target Lock will remain locked onto targets even if they move behind cover, allowing you to switch targets to a new enemy, or remain locked onto your original target when he peeks around the corner.

TARGET LOCK

Press and hold the Target Lock Button to pull out Neo's guns and make a crosshair appear over the target enemy. Using Target Lock increases Neo's accuracy and damage output.

Remember, a motionless target is a sitting duck. Be sure to use cover and keep moving continuously to avoid damage from enemy gunfire.

FOCUS SHOOTING

Holding the Focus Button while shooting dramatically increases Neo's accuracy and the damage he inflicts. Using Focus also allows Neo to move more quickly while firing, and he can avoid enemy bullets.

By combining Focus and Target Lock, Neo can target not only opponents but also dangerous elements in the environment, such as exploding gas cylinders, exploding barrels, blinding fire extinguishers and supports holding up platforms and pipes. If Neo does not target these environmental features immediately, use the Camera Control to move the targeting crosshair to the environmental object. Dangerous environmental explosives like the ones described in this paragraph can be identified easily using the Code Vision ability.

AMMUNITION

Neo can only fire weapons as long as he has ammunition remaining. When ammo runs out, the weapon disappears from his inventory screen. Neo replenishes ammo supplies by picking up additional weapons of the same type. For instance, picking up a Pistol refills Neo's supply of Pistol ammo. Ammunition remaining is displayed in the small window below the weapon window in the heads-up display.

DUAL WIELD

Certain weapons can be carried and fired two at a time, such as Pistols, Agent Pistols, and Submachine Guns (SMGs). Dual wielding weapons doubles Neo's rate of fire, with a slight drop in accuracy. When a weapon is dual wielded, the maximum ammo capacity Neo can carry is raised beyond the capacity of both guns combined.

FOCUS 360 AERIAL SHOOTING

With his amazing Focus abilities, the best place for Neo to be when firing is midair. Perform a Focus Jump or Wall Jump to get airborne, and then continue holding Focus as Neo flies and fires. While aloft, Neo can target enemies in every direction, not just in the direction to the front. When Neo fires during a jump, enemies have a much harder time shooting back with any success.

EVADE SHOTS

Try pressing the Evade Button while shooting and holding the Movement Control to the left or right to perform a "shoot dodge." When equipped with dual weapons, Neo performs a cool flip. But when equipped with an Assault Rifle or Grenade Launcher, he does a full cartwheel while firing. Neo is capable of firing with extreme accuracy during a cartwheel, and enemies will have a hard time hitting him with their shots.

KICK BACK

If enemies try to attack you when you're shooting, keep hammering the Fire Button - Neo will automatically perform a defensive power kick that knocks an enemy into the air. At this point, you can either continue blasting the enemy while they are airborne and vulnerable, or you can quickly release Target Lock and press Special Attack to initiate a Midair Grab or Tornado Throw. The Kick Back is possible only when Neo is firing a weapon.

BOSSES

Important enemies such as Agents and squad captains are much harder to fight than other foes. In the video game industry, such enemies are known as "bosses". Whenever a boss enemy is present, his or her life meter appears on the right side of the screen. Continue attacking boss enemies until their life gauge is depleted to defeat them.

Encountering a boss enemy means you should pull out all the stops. Use a Grenade Launcher or Fragmentation Grenades to cause severe damage to the boss, and make frequent if not incessant use of Focus. Although they are boss enemies, most of them can be eliminated with one or two highly extended hand-to-hand combos.

PATH OF THE ONE

"**When the Matrix was first built** there was a man born inside who had the ability to change whatever he wanted, to remake the Matrix as he saw fit. It was he who freed the first of us, taught us the truth; as long as the Matrix exists, the human race will never be free. After he died, the Oracle prophesied his return, and that his coming would hail the destruction of the Matrix, end the war, bring freedom to our people. That is why there are those of use who spent our lives searching the Matrix looking for him."

- Morpheus

To paraphrase the Oracle, being the One is like being in love; you either *know* you are the One, or you *don't* know. Uncertainty or confusion could lead to death, or worse, failure. By now, the Path of the One is well known from the film series. However, players should find that the game illuminates the difference between what it means to know a path and what it means to *walk* that path. <u>**The Matrix: Path of Neo**</u> takes place partially within the events of the films, but also broadens the scope of action and expands the boundaries of this familiar tale. This section of the guide erases all uncertainty.

THE WACHOWSKI BROTHERS AND SHINY COMMENTARY

Throughout the walkthrough, you'll find boxes identifying commentary and conceptual sections on how the game was envisioned, what it was meant to be, and, in some cases, what was changed (or even left out) in the finished product.
This is a rare insight into the development of a game and into the thought processes behind the creation of the property and its use. Take advantage of these sections to find out even more about The Matrix: Path of Neo.

THE WACHOWSKI BROTHERS' CONCEPT

The path of this game will parallel the evolution of Neo's consciousness, graduating from gross to subtle to casual states of awareness, culminating, as all journeys to higher consciousness do, with a battle against a monster (in this case, MegaSmith).

Overall, the structure of the game will be similar to ETM alternating between gameplay and edited film scenes. Stylistically, the film footage will be reduced to shorthand; bare bones and rapid fire montage that try to focus on the ideas that one must Special Attack with on their path.

We do like the idea of adding the RPG element in the form of "skill tiles," however, we would suggest that one of the skills be called something like "awareness" or "atman" and that the selection of these tiles would seem to give you nothing more than meaningless koan-like expressions such as, "you can hear the sound of one hand clapping," but in fact, this skill secretly gives enormous bonuses to your other skills. We also feel that you should be constantly earning awareness or atman points and that these points allow you to buy or upgrade skills.

Besides "focus," we imagine there should be a skill that allows you to create a force-field bubble around yourself which would deflect or stop bullets (perhaps the Defend Button creates a shimmering translucent sphere that automatically blocks any projectile--in "focus" you could watch them all stopping dead as they hit your shield.) Telekinesis is a skill Neo demonstrates which might be developed into some interesting game play.

"Neo is the standard against which every player must be measured.
It is the goal of this game to illuminate the difference between what it means to know a path and what it means to walk that path."

SHINY'S COMMENTARY

The concept of the player continually upgrading his or her character with skills was something that was planned for Enter the Matrix. It was a natural fit in a world where you could "download" new skills into your brain.

For this game, though, the skill tree took on a focus of Neo's growth toward higher consciousness. So the skills were divided into three parts - the Special and Master Abilities, and the higher level Atman Principles.

EVER HAD A DREAM, NEO?

"Have you ever had a dream,
Neo, that you were so sure was real? What if you were
unable to wake from that dream? How would you know
the difference between the dream world and the real
world?"

- Morpheus

OBJECTIVES

Defeat as many enemies as possible.

OPPONENTS

Security Guard

Police

SHAT

Riot Police

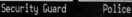
Agent Jones

Tiger Vamp

Agent Smith

AVAILABLE WEAPONS

Pistol

Heavy Pistol

SMG

Assault Rifle

TAKE THE RED PILL

Neo's path starts with the simplest of choices. Use the Movement control to move the camera towards Morpheus' hand that is holding the red pill, and press the Accept/Jump Button to take it from him. For all purposes, taking the blue pill is merely a quick way to *end* the game, which is not as interesting as *playing* the game.

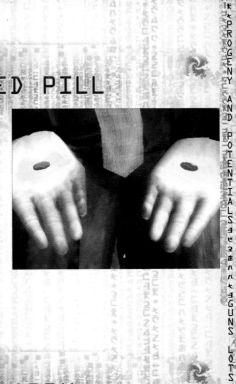

THE DREAM LOBBY

Quite unlike what you may remember from the film, Neo finds himself in a dreamlike building lobby. This is a challenge level designed to determine the player's level of gaming ability. If Neo can survive longer and defeat more enemies, more and greater difficulty levels become unlocked. The greater the enemy, the more hand-to-hand combination moves Neo shall have at his disposal.

After a few moments, Security Guards emerge from the elevators at the top of the room. The guards are unarmed, so it should be no problem to defeat them with a few hand-to-hand combat moves. When a Security Guard approaches within close range, press the Strike Button to attack them. Press the Strike Button again at the instant the first blow lands to initiate a combination attack.

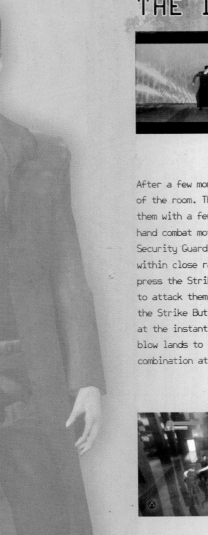

Continue punching and kicking the Security Guard until he glows briefly as if short-circuiting, which means he is defeated. Then move the Movement control toward the next Security Guard, and take him down in the same manner.

DISARMING ENEMIES

Soon after both Security Guards lie motionless, two Police officers enter the lobby with guns drawn. Neo resumes play in the middle of the lobby, exposed and out in the open. Move immediately left or right to the columns to take cover, then weave around them while making your way toward the Police.

Neo can take weapons and firearms away from armed enemies. To disarm an opponent, approach within a few feet while they still have their gun drawn. Press the Strike Button once or twice to hit the opponent, then press the Special Attack Button to knock them off balance. When the Fire Button icon appears onscreen, press the button to perform a Weapon Strip. The enemy drops their weapon, allowing Neo to pick it up and use it.

ARM YOURSELF

Neo must rely on weapons he can find or take from enemies. Weapon Strips are the best strategy for disarming enemies and turning them back on their owners. Enemies often holster their weapons when engaging Neo in hand-to-hand combat, so the secret is open attacks with a Weapon Strip. At higher levels, the Weapon Strip moves are also cool finishers that can damage surrounding enemies.
Another great tactic is to back off just enough for the enemy to redraw their weapon. This allows you another chance to perform a Weapon Strip on them and get their weapons.

"ARE YOU TRYING TO SAY I CAN DODGE BULLETS?"

A heavily armed SWAT team floods the lobby next. Armed foes immediately open fire when at great distances from their target. Move behind the columns to either side of Neo and use these obstructions for cover while working your way toward the SWAT guys. To reduce the amount of damage Neo takes from automatic fire, hold the Focus Button while moving. In Focus mode, bullets fired from enemy weapons move more slowly, leaving visible bullet waves in the air. Neo moves faster in Focus mode. Focus makes it easier to see the path of projectiles and to move out of harm's way.

While moving toward the SWAT guys, hold the Target Lock Button and press the Fire Button to shoot back. You can pick off enemies, and the SWAT team will likely scurry for cover, giving you time to reach the group for more effective hand-to-hand attacks. Use Focus while running and shooting to improve aiming accuracy. Press the Evade Button to flip to the side while shooting, or press Jump to leap toward foes while firing, making Neo harder to hit.

Move in for close combat with SWAT members as soon as possible. When Neo fights hand-to-hand with a SWAT guy, all other enemies stop firing. Try to use Weapon Strip moves to take Submachine Guns and Assault Rifles away from SWAT guys. Otherwise, take them down as fast as possible. Hit them with a few Strikes, and use Special Attack to trigger throws and other combinations. You can use the Movement controls to direct your throws - try throwing enemies in the direction of other enemies to knock them down.

FINISH THEM OFF!

Try mixing combinations with Focus to perform powerful and visually impressive finishing moves, such as Neo's trademark high kick. Also finish off enemies by pressing and holding the Special Attack Button for three seconds to gather energy, and then release the button to unleash a Killing Blow.

SHIELDED FOES

Riot Police enter the lobby next. Tougher and more defensively oriented than SWAT, Riot Police require a greater number of hits to defeat. While fighting one Riot officer, other active Riot Police surround and attack Neo from behind. Avoid being surrounded by using the Evade Button in combination with the Movement control to spin out of the center of the circle.

Two of the Riot Police carry shields, which they use to defend against attacks and to bash Neo in the face. If Neo is knocked down or flung through the air, press the Evade Button before landing to get back up quickly. The Riot officers can be made to drop their shields, by continuously punching and kicking them or by using Evade moves to flank the Riot Police and attacking from behind. An attack from the rear may cause them to drop their shields instantaneously.

Riot Police are much stronger in hand-to-hand combat than previously encountered enemy types. Block the blows of a Riot Police enemy by pressing the Strike Button at the same instant he attempts to punch or kick. After blocking several attempted blows, the officer may become stunned and that Neo's attacks are less likely to be blocked. It also means that Neo can more easily attack multiple opponents successfully. So if Riot Police surround Neo and one or more of them is stunned, use the Movement Control to direct each successive Strike or Special Attack toward a different opponent.

Neo can also be stunned, either by missing attacks or taking too much damage too quickly. If Neo gets stunned, hammer Evade several times to quickly snap out of it. Defeat at least one of the Riot Police to unlock the Master (Normal) difficulty level.

"IT'S AN AGENT!"

Hope you have some health remaining, because Agent Jones is one tough customer. Use the columns for cover while moving toward the Agent to avoid his fire. Approach within close range and he will holster his weapon. Avoid moving too far from the Agent, or he'll redraw his weapon and continue firing. As you shall learn quickly, Neo can't absorb many bullets from a Heavy Pistol.

Agents are much stronger and faster martial artists than other foes. They're also harder to hit with Special Attacks and Combos, and are capable of reversing attempts to grapple or stun them. Use Focus to slow the action, making it easier to block strikes and counterattack. Strike the Agent a few times, then press the Special Attack Button when the appropriate button icon appears onscreen. Follow this up with the subsequent commands shown to inflict as much damage on Agent Jones with one combo as possible.

If too many of Neo's attacks are blocked and he becomes stunned, use Evade moves to back off. Allow Focus and health to recharge slightly by moving just far enough to stand off against the Agent, but not far enough for him to redraw his gun.

THE EXILE

Neo then encounters one of the bizarre programs existing within the Matrix known as an "Exile". These enemies display uncanny talents equal to and above Neo's such as walking on ceilings. When the Exile appears, use automatic weapons and Focus to drive him down to the ground. Block his strikes in hand-to-hand, and do not hesitate to be more evasive than usual. The Exile can easily block and evade many of Neo's attacks, which can temporarily stun Neo. Use Focused Strikes to make him stagger, then follow up by using the controls displayed onscreen.

During this contest Neo becomes capable of an aerial slamming move. After striking and then grappling the Exile, hold the Focus Button and press Jump to grab the Exile and crash into the ceiling. Then Neo switches positions with the foe midair and slams their head into the ground underfoot. Perform this action as many times as possible to inflict high amounts of damage to the Exile in the hopes of defeating him.

Neo's final challenge to determine his level of ability pits him against none other than his nemesis, Agent Smith. Button mashing is not sufficient for this match. Use Focus to dodge his gunfire and move in close. Then block his blows by matching Strikes until some of Neo's Focus meter has recharged. When Smith is significantly damaged, he uses any opportunity to seize Neo for a finishing blow, such as his chest-pounding Fist Bouquet. Use Evade frequently to avoid being seized and finished off with this humiliating attack. Charge your blows with Focus and attack him from the side or flank as much as possible. If you can beat Smith, Neo emerges as the One. This unlocks the hard difficulty mode. The game certainly makes you fight for this honor!

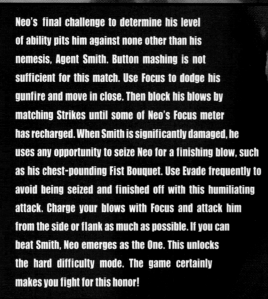

AGENT SMITH

CLASS:

AGENT

SPECIAL ABILITIES:

BULLET DODGE

FIST BOUQUET

THE WACHOWSKI BROTHERS' VISION

To begin, a player should first choose a red pill. The screen should then rain-drop away, leaving darkness from which we hear a voice as though it was in our head, "Have you ever had a dream you were so sure was real?" A pile-driver sound effect slams us into a bright dream-like version of the Government Lobby.

It is not the actual location but a symbolic representation of it; the edges are lost in fog, the end always recedes towards infinity. As Neo, the player faces the basic progression of foes from the matrix: Security guard-to-cop-to-s.w.a.t. dude-to-soldier-to-agent-to-exile-to-agent smith. Above the music and effects the player will be bombarded by a super-condensed dialogue track from the three films, flutter-cut together into a gatling gun spray of juxtaposing ideas. As the action gets more furious, so does the onslaught of this track.

If the player dies, his progress is ranked and the difficulty of their path chosen i.e. novice, disciple, master and lastly, if you make it all the way, "You're path is the Path of the One." This should be as repeatable as many times as the player wants if a harder difficulty is desired.

FILM FOOTAGE

(Film montages will act as the bridges in between gameplay. However, certain moments during play require short segues between the action to cover the gaps in the narrative. These short beats will be assessed later for whether film footage or a quick animatic makes sense.)

The images come fast with an array of inter-cut, intermingling, dialogue floating ethereally above.

A trace program. "She got out." Follow the white rabbit. "What is the Matrix?"

SHINY'S COMMENTARY

Like how their films are constructed, the Wachowski Brothers divided the game into specific story "beats," and then Shiny divided those beats into specific game levels.

The "film footage" descriptions were a little puzzling at first, because we had no idea what the Wachowski Brothers and film editor Zach Staenberg really had in mind when they wrote "bare bones and rapid-fire montage."

When the first film cuts were delivered, we had a serious "whoa" moment when we realized that what the Wachowski Brothers were really creating was a "director's cut" of the entire trilogy.

THEY'RE COMING FOR YOU, NEO

OBJECTIVES

Escape from MetaCortech:
- Follow Morpheus' instructions.

- Get to the office and climb outside.

Bonus Objective
- Complete your escape without getting captured.

OPPONENTS

Security Guard   Police

"I've been looking for you.
I don't know if you're ready to see what I want to show you, but unfortunately, you and I have run out of time. They're coming for you, Neo, and I don't know what they're going to do."
- Morpheus

HARD DAY AT THE OFFICE

Ordinary 'Joe-Schmo' Thomas Anderson is sitting quietly in his office when Agents and Police arrive to arrest him. At this point, Anderson is still plugged into the Matrix and doesn't know it. He does not have any hand-to-hand combat abilities or weapons knowledge. The goal is to sneak out of the office building without being detected. If Anderson is seized and held by Security Guards or Police long enough, he is captured. The game then asks if you wish to accept capture or retry. Accepting capture ends the stage immediately, but the action still progresses to the next stage. Try to alter the Path of Neo by exiting the building and reaching the street level, where Trinity waits on her motorcycle.

With Morpheus' voice in your ear, move from Anderson's cubicle to the one across the row. Navigate toward the highlighted area and press the Action Button to Link-Up with the wall. Wait for Morpheus' next command, and then use the Movement Control to peel Anderson's back off the cubicle divider and head up the row behind the receding Police officer.

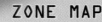

GOT PINNED?

Police and Security Guards will not attack Anderson, but they do try to seize his wrist and pin his arm behind him. Rapidly tap the Strike Button to break free of this hold before too much time elapses, or the game will consider Anderson to be captured!

RAT IN A MAZE

Slowly follow the highlighted officer until Morpheus tells Anderson to hide behind another cubicle wall. This is to avoid being spotted by the Security Guard in the aisle, who is about to turn. Wait for Morpheus' next piece of advice, and then move into the highlighted cubicle and Link-Up with the low wall.

ROLLING IN THE AISLES

After Morpheus guides Anderson back out to the main aisle, Link-Up with the highlighted wall. Push the Movement Control toward the corner to make Anderson lean out slightly, and then press the Jump Button to perform a dodge roll across the aisle to the opposite corner.

As the officer continues up the narrow corridor, follow him and Link-Up with the edge of the file cabinet on the right side of the passage. When the Police officer gets to the corner, move across the corridor and Link-Up with the wall. Tilt the Movement Control diagonally to make Anderson move along the wall to the corner, where the conversation between the Security Guard and the officer can be overheard.

ZONE MAP

ASSISTANCE

When Morpheus says so, step out from the wall and move swiftly around the curved desk. Be sure to move along the desk very closely or Anderson could be spotted and attacked. Go behind the desk and hide in the indicated corner by Link-Up with the filing cabinet. Do not worry about the office assistant, because it just so happens she thinks Anderson is cute and feigns ignorance regarding these antics.

THE OFFICE AT THE END OF THE CORRIDOR

After Smith questions the assistant and moves off, wait for Morpheus' cue and then head down the hall and around the corner. Stay behind the highlighted Police officer. Link-Up with the corners to get a better view of the next passage.

At the final corner, Anderson's boss emerges from his office and stands in the doorway. As Morpheus indicates, all that Anderson can do is make a dash for the office. Move around the corner and the Policeman will rush at Anderson. Preempt his impending Special Attack by pressing the Strike Button to shove the Policeman to the ground. Quickly race into the executive's office.

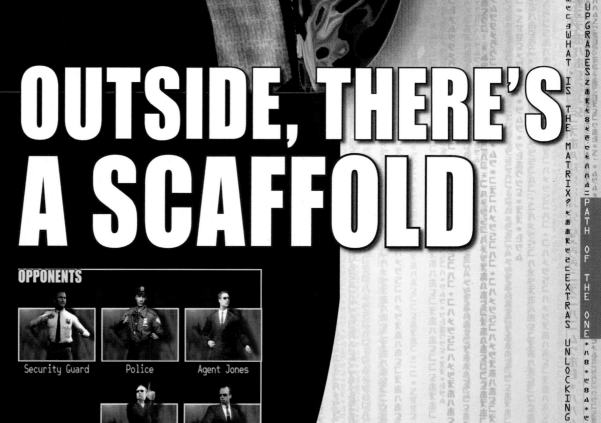

OUTSIDE, THERE'S A SCAFFOLD

OBJECTIVES

Escape from MetaCortech:
- Get to the roof and enter the building.

- Once inside, head down to the delivery exit.

Look-Up: Move near a wall and press

Bonus Objective:
- Complete your escape without getting captured.

OPPONENTS

Security Guard   Police   Agent Jones

Agent Brown   Agent Smith

STAGE MAP

ZONE MAP

Continue sidestepping down the thin ledge until Anderson suddenly loses his balance and falls to a hanging position. Press the Jump Button to release the edge and drop onto the cargo lift below. The lift engages and rises to the next level. Press the Jump Button to climb up to the ledge and continue sidestepping around the building toward the two scaffolds parked on the level.

Ignore the Police officer who spots Anderson, and move onto the lift with the flashing green control light. Position Anderson in front of the switch and press the Action Button to raise the scaffold.

WEATHERING HEIGHTS

On the perilous ledges surrounding the building, the mechanics are a bit different. Move around the corner from the starting position and Anderson automatically does a Link-Up with the wall in order to cross the thin section. Use the Movement Controls to work your way down the ledge until Anderson encounters an obstruction. Step away from the wall, move to the edge and continue holding the Movement Control down until Anderson climbs down to a hanging position. Shimmy along the ledge until Anderson is past the structural support. Then tilt the Movement Control upward to make Anderson climb back up onto the ledge.

ZONE MAP

Follow the plank back onto the building ledge, and approach the officer at the corner. After an "incident", wait at the corner for a construction worker to stop the rising scaffold at Anderson's level. Board the scaffold; the worker agrees to head for the upper floors of the building.

ZONE MAP

WATCH YOUR STEP, OFFICER

When Agents override the scaffold's controls and leave Anderson stuck between levels, the only option is to move to the opening in the bars and drop onto the wooden platform. Anderson crashes through the wood to the level below, and a Police officer is already descending the nearby ladder.

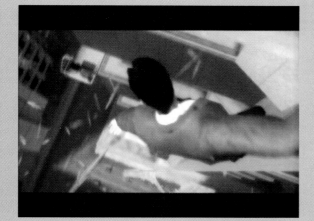

Tilt the Movement Control upward to climb onto the wooden platform Anderson dangles from, and quickly rush toward the ladder. Press the Strike Button to topple the Policeman. Climb the ladder to the upper level and race toward the edge. Press the Jump Button as Anderson approaches the ledge to leap the gap in the wooden platforms.

TOP OF THE WORLD

A Police officer is waiting on the sixteenth floor. Ignore his threats and shimmy across the ledge. Do not worry about the Agent waiting in the doorway at the end. When Anderson reaches that point, he automatically loses balance and falls over the edge. Press the Jump Button to drop onto the cargo lift below, which raises him to the rooftop.

Drop from the cargo container onto the rooftop and move toward the left door. Press the Action Button to open it. Anderson suddenly finds himself in the grip of a Security Guard. Rapidly tap the Strike Button to break free, and then push down the Security Guard and Police. Quickly go through the door to get away from the System's advocates.

HE'S HEADING FOR THE STREET

"This is insane! Why is this happening to me? What'd I do? I'm nobody. I didn't do anything. I'm gonna die."
- Neo

OBJECTIVES

Escape from MetaCortech.

Bonus Objective:
- Complete your escape without getting captured.

OPPONENTS

Security Guard

Police

Agent Brown

Agent Smith

Agent Jones

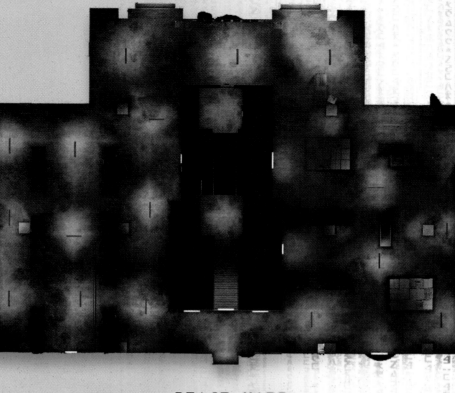

STAGE MAPS

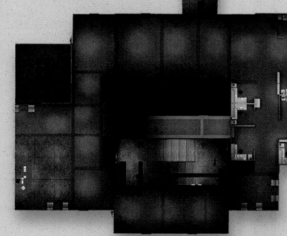

ZONE MAP

THE BIG O

Descend the stairs. A map of the level is posted on the wall directly opposite the bottom step. Look at it a moment to get your bearings. Anderson must cross through the entire level and get to the exit door on the other side.

Head to Anderson's right and go around the corner. Move along the shelves to the left and Link-Up with the end of a row so that the Police officer patrolling the area beyond can be seen. Wait until he turns left and walks behind the shelves; step out and head down the aisle to the end. Race around the corner and press the Strike Button to topple the Police officer blocking the door. Press the Action Button to quickly open the door before any of the Police can seize Anderson.

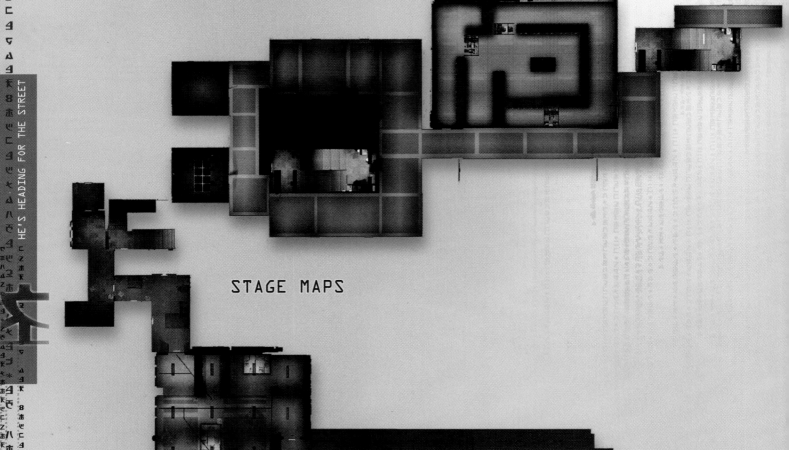

STAGE MAPS

ZONE MAP

ZONE MAP

ZONE MAP

POLICE BREAK

Descend the stairs to the 12th floor. This is the only exit that is not blocked or guarded by Police. Upon exiting, turn to the right and follow the Police officer who just announced to the world that he is headed for the john. Stop at the corner just past the elevators, Link-Up to the wall, and peek into the next area. Wait for the officer to go inside the restroom, and then continue into the cubicle area.

HEAD ABOVE WALLS

Move Anderson up to the corner of the row of cubicles, but not far enough that you lose sight of the officer patrolling underneath the large red 'EXIT' sign. Stay at the bottom corner of the cubicles until he turns and begins to head down the row to the right away from the exit. Quickly head up the right aisle and run down the exit corridor. Press Action to go through the door at the end.

SERVER ROOM CHASE

Run down the flights of stairs to level six. Just a few feet into the level, Anderson encounters Agent Smith and a squad of Police, waiting for him in the corridor. As soon as the dialog ends, dash through the door on the right and into the server room. Head to the right and race down the rows of equipment to the opening. Then continue to the back of the room and race through the open doorway.

OPERATOR HERE:
Watch the Server Room Exit Door!

A Police officer may come through the top doorway, so be ready to knock him down when moving past the last row of servers.

HOLD THAT DOOR

Upon exiting the server room, head down the passage and around the corner to the right. As you race down to the end, a Security Guard opens the exit door. Press the Strike Button to knock down the guard, and go through the door.

ZONE MAP

BOTTOM LEVEL

The Security Guard and Police from level six pursue Anderson down the stairs, so do not stop for any reason. An officer on the bottom level across from the stair landing already has his gun drawn. Do not stop for a moment. If you stop and then continue moving again, he will fire and probably kill you. Instead, continue running around the corner to the left and through the doorway marked with a red 'EXIT' sign. Curve to the right while going through the next room and head through the next doorway.

ZONE MAP

ITCHY TRIGGER FINGER

ZONE MAP

A Police officer at the far end of the package area also has his weapon drawn. Do not move too closely to this frightened officer, or he will open fire and kill Anderson. Instead, proceed into the room and then run left around the corner of the shelves. Head for the doorway with the glowing red 'EXIT' sign and weave into the next area.

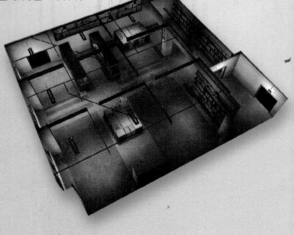

ZONE MAP

TRINITY AWAITS!

Although it looks like a clear shot from this point to the exit door, stay wary when approaching the daylight. A Security Guard smashes through the boxes on the left, and has a good chance of seizing Anderson. Press the Strike Button rapidly if needed to break free and then dash for the exit and Trinity.

Unlock Level Concept Art!

Reach Trinity waiting on her motorbike without being captured to unlock Level Concept Art files in the Media Viewer!

> "Without any **combat** experience as of yet in the timeline, this will be mainly a stealth mission and any option for combat must result in a quick knockout or the player's opponent will call for help."

THE WACHOWSKI BROTHERS' VISION

The path of the "one" begins with Thomas Anderson trying to escape the Agents, guided by Morpheus' voice through the corporate rat maze.

The office itself is a Seussian labyrinth of cubicles that seem to stretch to the horizon. The player must not only avoid the pursuing Agents, police and security guards, Thomas Anderson's fellow office drones will fink him out on site. If at any time the player is caught, they are taken away by the Agents and the next film montage begins.

If the player survives the high winds on the window ledge and scaffold, (perhaps in an animatic the phone is blown from your hand suggesting the danger of the winds; the player can then give up as Neo did or continue on.

If you make it to the scaffold, Smith sees you through the window heading for the roof, which begins a mad dash down though the entire length of Cortechs, weaving in and out of the rabbit warren of duct work, down elevator shafts and across floors of cubicled mazes. If the player reaches the delivery exit, they will find Trinity waiting on her motorcycle.

Dispatching an Agent or even a cop at this point, should be near impossible.

FILM FOOTAGE

(Note: If the player is able to evade the Agents, a truncated montage will play, with Trinity racing away to Morpheus and the Lafayette.)

A choice. Awake. Heal. The dark truth.

KUNG FU TRAINING

> "Jujitsu? I'm going to learn jujitsu?
> - Neo

OBJECTIVES

Complete the hand-to-hand combat training program.

Complete all training programs to unlock a Bonus Award.

OPPONENTS

Kung Fu Soldier

Master Sting (BOSS)

AVAILABLE WEAPON

Short Stick°

*Depends on completion of extra criteria.

STAGE MAP

ZONE MAP

ZONE MAP

SILENT TAKEDOWNS

Free from the Matrix, Neo must now undergo intensive combat and weapons training to become a member of the *Nebuchadnezzar* crew. The skills introduced in these simulation stages go a long way toward determining whether Neo is up to the task of becoming the One. Each of these training programs look like they're inspired by famous action films. The Kung Fu Training level, for instance, is loosely influenced by 70s karate films such as <u>Enter the Dragon</u>.

After Neo and The Operator work out a few kinks in the equipment, move slowly and quietly up behind the nearby Kung Fu Soldier, whose back is turned. When Neo stands just a step or two behind the man, press and hold the Special Attack Button to seize the man's head in a sleeper hold and knock him unconscious. If you fail to execute a Silent Takedown, the Operator resets the program one time so that you may try again.

A TREE FALLS IN THE FOREST

Perform Silent Takedowns on the two Kung Fu fighters in the corridor, and proceed to the storage room. It's time now to start working on hand-to-hand combos. Face one of the two Kung Fu Soldiers in the room and Neo enters the hand-to-hand combat stance. If you begin wildly pressing the Strike Button, the enemy can probably block all your attacks. Allow them to attempt the first strike. Block their attacks by pressing Strike, and continue pressing Strike to counterattack. Button icons may appear onscreen. Press the associated control to Special Attack and then finish off enemies with a devastating series of moves.

Continue fighting the Kung Fu Soldiers spawned by the Operator until the room is clear. Smash the small wood crates scattered around the room if needed to pick up **Health Packs.**

ZONE MAP

LEARN MULTI-OPPONENT TACTICS

Neo's hand-to-hand moves during this training simulation are more stylized and basic than usual, in keeping with the theme of the level. However, this should not stop you from trying to initiate multi-opponent combos. To fight more than one enemy simultaneously, move the Movement Control toward one enemy and press Strike, and then tilt the Movement Control toward another enemy and press Strike. Now that both enemies are reeling, Special Attack one and then the other. Finally, press Strike again to initiate a spectacular looking multi-opponent combo.

KUNG FU TRAINING

ZONE MAP

ZONE MAP

ZONE MAP

CONTROL ROOM CHALLENGE

The Operator wants Neo to sneak into the control room undetected. This means entering the enclosed area without being spotted and preventing either the two guards from triggering the alarm by pushing the button on the wall near the door. If this is accomplished, the Operator hacks the next area to insert a Short Stick for Neo to use in combat.

Move along the wall to the left, and then follow the control room wall around to the ramp on the side. Enter the room and engage the two men in hand-to-hand. You must take on both simultaneously, otherwise either man left unattended immediately runs for the alarm. If the alarm is sounded, additional Kung Fu Soldiers appear and attack.

TRIPLE STEALTH TAKEDOWN

Three Kung Fu Soldiers are practicing their chops on tables in the tool shop. All have their backs turned, so it is possible to take out all three

silently. Sneak up behind the Soldier in white nearest the entrance and press Special Attack to take him down, and then do the same for the other man dressed in white to the left. Finally, take down the Kung Fu Soldier dressed in red.

Unlock Staff Combos Video!

Take down all three Kung Fu Soldiers in the tool shop with silent kills. A briefcase appears near the alarm on the wall. Collect the suitcase to unlock a video in the Making Of portion of the Extras menu. This video highlights many of the super cool moves Neo can perform when equipped with a staff.

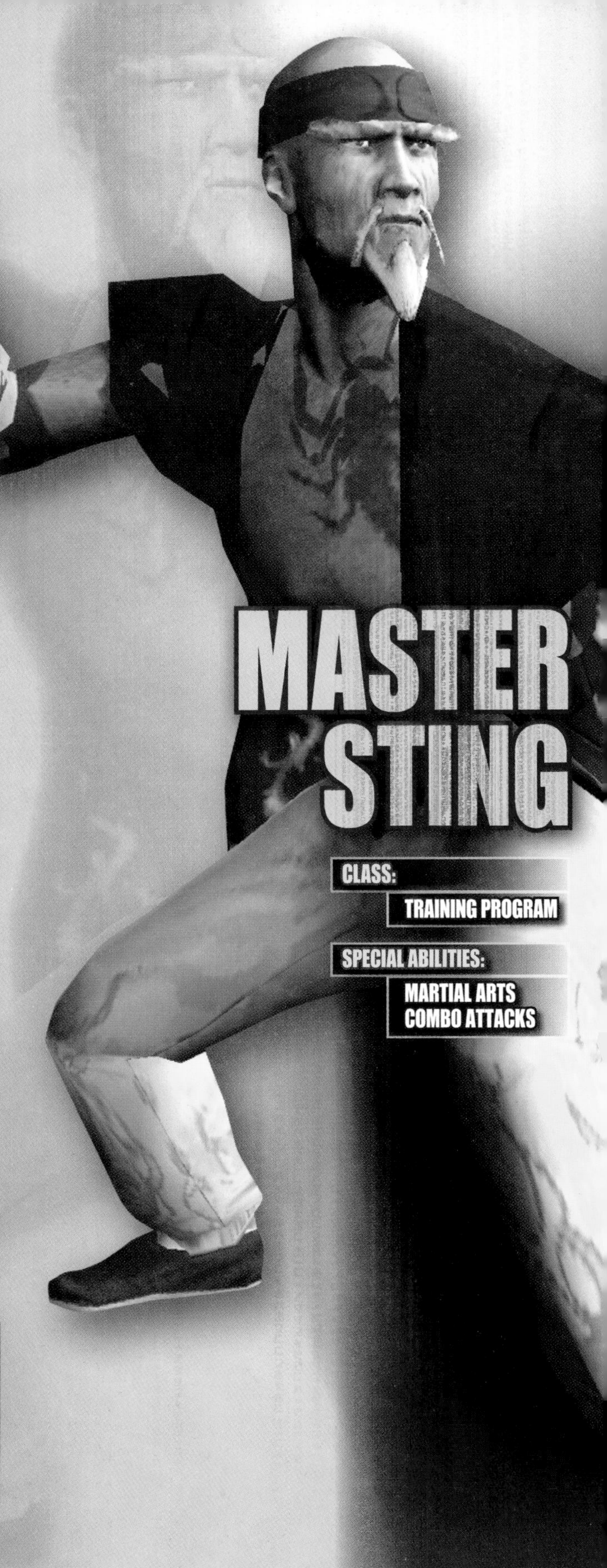

LAVA PIT LEAP

Move cautiously through the next corridor, pressing the Jump Button while running to leap over magma-filled pits. The second pit is a bit wider than the first, but with the proper jump timing Neo should be able to grab the opposite ledge and hoist himself up. Continue down the corridor, take down the lone inept guard at the end and climb the ladder.

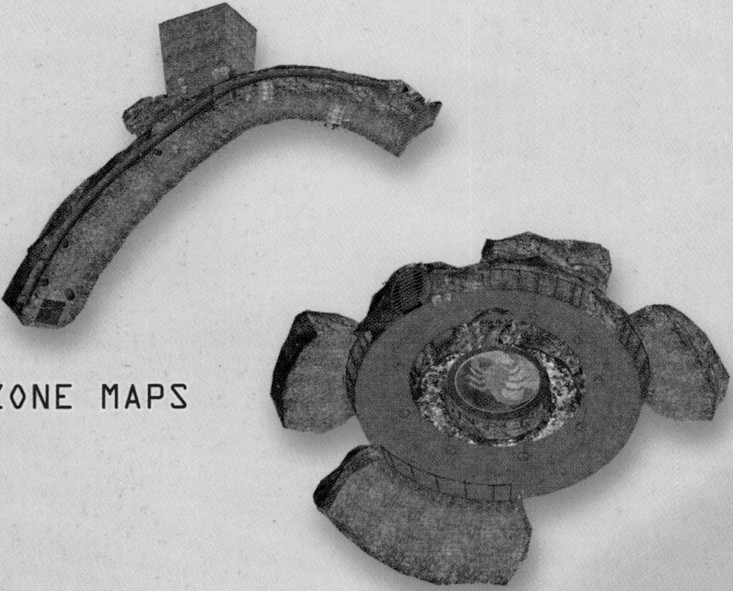

ZONE MAPS

MASTER STING

CLASS:

TRAINING PROGRAM

SPECIAL ABILITIES:

MARTIAL ARTS COMBO ATTACKS

TOURNAMENT BATTLE

Use Multi-Opponent strategies as described in the previous tip to take on three Kung Fu Soldiers at once. Knock opponents over the side of the ring into the boiling hot "mag-MAH" to eliminate them instantly. Each subsequent wave of foes should prove to be better at blocking and counterattacking than the previous, so use Evade moves to snap out of stun and avoid hits.

After defeating the first wave, Neo gains the Focus ability. However, the meter is extremely tiny, and Focus is fleeting. Punch through an enemy's defenses first, and then use Focus to help finish them off stylishly.

The Path of Neo

Following Neo's first training session, the Path of Neo becomes visible for the first time. In this stylized menu, upgrades can be acquired to enhance Neo's abilities and new skills can be learned. At this point, there are no new upgrades available. However, you should take a moment to examine the multiple rings of the Path, using the cursor to highlight unlearned skills to determine what lies ahead.

The Kung Fu master is extremely defensive, blocking most Strikes delivered head on. The key is to use Evade in combination with the Movement Control to reposition Neo behind Master Sting, and ambush him. Use Focus to strike him and continue holding the Focus Button and try to turn the event into a powerful combo with additional Strikes and Special Attacks. Repeat this strategy until Master Sting is defeated.

Avoid the sides of the tournament ring, or Master Sting may knock Neo into the surrounding magma for additional damage. When stun clouds swirl around Neo's head, use Evade to back away and recoup rather than try to sneak attack. Master Sting launches into a modified, inescapable Killing Blow that drains Neo's minimal health severely. He does not hesitate to perform this action any time Neo shows the slightest sign of weakness in form.

OBJECTIVES

Defeat the Swordsman.

Bonus Objective:
- Complete all training programs to unlock a Bonus Award.

OPPONENT

Swordsman (BOSS)

AVAILABLE WEAPON

Katana

SWORD TRAINING

"We're supposed to start with these operation programs first. That's major boring. Let's do something more fun. How about combat training?"

- Tank

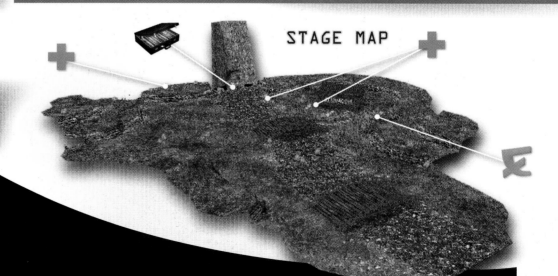

STAGE MAP

The Swordsman is a program designed to help Neo hone his melee weapon abilities. He is based on characters appearing in Japanese anime films such as <u>Ninja Scroll</u>. While engaged in hand-to-hand combat, the Swordsman can attempt a Blade Charge attack. During this attack, he focuses his energy on his blade and then lashes out with a powerful thrust. This is a modified Killing Blow move capable of knocking Neo to the ground. He can also blind Neo by reflecting the sun's light from his sword. While Neo is blinded, the screen is temporarily filled with light. The Swordsman often attempts this attack if Neo attempts to charge a Killing Blow.

To defeat the Swordsman, Neo must evade his normal sword strike attempts and attack him from the side or behind. Use Special Attack moves to stun the Swordsman, and then press the Strike Button to begin a sword combo attack. When the Swordsman conjures doppelganger clones of himself, engage the doppelgangers one at a time until the true Swordsman is discovered. Keep your eye on the boss's life gauge on the side of the screen. When you see that you or Trinity have reduced the gauge with attacks, keep attacking that particular clone.

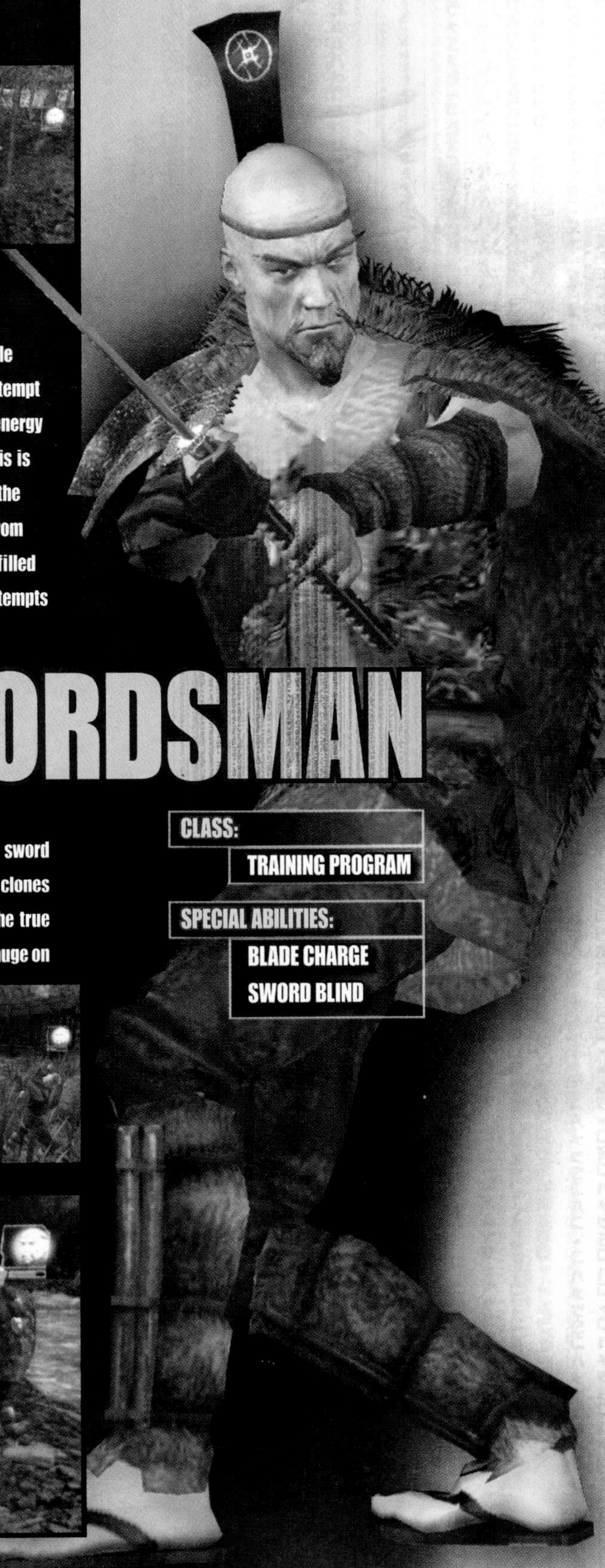

SWORDSMAN

CLASS:

TRAINING PROGRAM

SPECIAL ABILITIES:

BLADE CHARGE

SWORD BLIND

Unlock Sword Combos Video!

Before or during the battle with the Swordsman, go through the waterfall at the far end of the stream and smash the pots to reveal a briefcase. Pickup the briefcase to unlock this video of cool sword moves in the Making Of menu!

The Path of Neo

Notice that Neo obtains the 4 Hit Combo during his battle with the Swordsman. Neo's standard combination attack is one Strike longer than it was before, allowing him to do more damage to a foe in rapid succession!

OBJECTIVES

Complete melee weapon training program.

- Defeat all enemies and find a way out of the pagoda.

- Locate and defeat Ogami the spirit to learn Killing Blow.

- Defeat all enemies in the winter garden.

WINTER TRAINING

Bonus Objective:
- Complete all training programs to unlock a Bonus Award.

OPPONENTS

Demon Ninja (BOSS)

Ogami (BOSS)

Japanese Assassin

AVAILABLE WEAPON

Katana

"Good morning. Did you sleep? You will tonight, I guarantee it."
- Tank

STAGE MAP

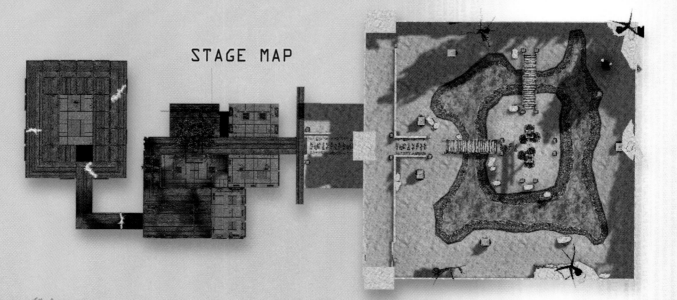

CHILLING VECTORS

Although Neo is ready to continue his training, something is wrong with the simulator and ghosts have entered the machine. Collect the **Katana** from the rack at the top of the room and chop through the door on either side of the room. Continue slashing through sliding doors and try to find a way out to the corridor.

ZONE MAP

The samurai spirit of Ogami appears in the corridor. Slash through additional sliding doors and follow the apparition out to the passage. The specter opens a chasm in the floor. Touching this chasm drains Neo's life. The best way to get across the chasm is by performing a Wall Run. Accomplish this by holding the Focus Button while running parallel along a wall. Continue holding Focus as Neo runs up onto the wall and over the chasm.

Pursue Ogami into the next passage, and Wall Run again to cross the glowing chasm. This time, you must gauge the arc of the Wall Run so that Neo does

not touch the green light erupting from the wall. At the final corner, Neo must Wall Run over both a glowing chasm and a lantern. If Neo touches the lantern during the Wall Run, it explodes and causes him damage.

ZONE MAP

PRACTICE ROOM

Chop through the sliding doors at the top of the chamber and proceed across the hallway to a training room to take on additional samurai. When fighting surrounding enemies with a sword, the idea is to fight one enemy while occasionally delivering an offline slash to an opponent to the side of or behind Neo. When the swordsmen are defeated, collect the many Katana hung on the racks surrounding the room and return to the corridor. Slash through the sliding doors at the corner to find Ogami waiting patiently.

LYING IN WAIT

Proceed up the long corridor and Wall Run over a final glowing chasm in the floor. Approach the double doors to encounter a group of Japanese Assassins, waiting for Neo. Fight them with the same sword techniques used in the previous training, only this time work on Multi-Opponent fighting with a sword. Try to knock opponents into the exploding lanterns surrounding the room for instant kills. Smash the tall wardrobe on the side of the room to reveal a **Health Pack** if needed. But while chopping up the furniture, avoid striking any of the exploding lanterns in the corners of the room.

OGAMI

CLASS:

TRAINING PROGRAM

SPECIAL ABILITIES:

BLADE CHARGE

Ogami is a little more difficult than are the previously encountered Assassins in the stage. Use Focus to begin your sword-slicing combos, and allow Neo to take it from there. After successfully Striking Ogami a few times, press the Special Attack Button to stun him and then Strike again to initiate a triple spin-slice attack. Try to drive and kick Ogami toward one of the exploding lanterns in two corners of the chamber to inflict major damage. A health item sits in the corner if required.

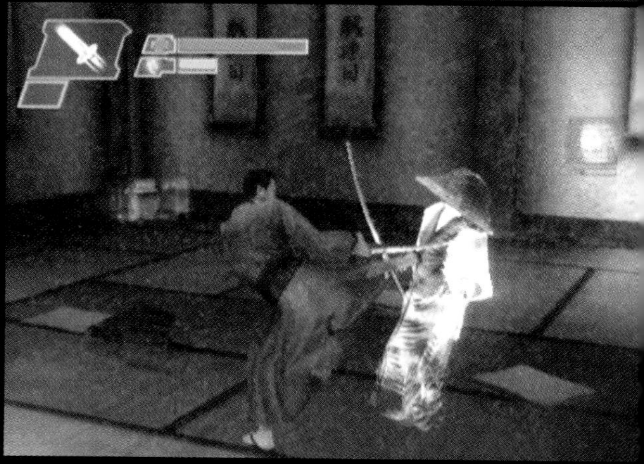

THE KILLING BLOW

After defeating Ogami, wait for a few comments from the Operator and then approach the open cabinet in the samurai spirit's chamber. Take the scroll within the container to learn the Killing Blow technique and extend the Focus meter. To perform a Killing Blow with the equipped melee weapon or hand-to-hand, hold the Focus Button and Special Attack Buttons to charge up power. Rippling wave effects begin to surround Neo. When ready, release the Special Attack Button to launch forward, thrusting into and through an enemy. Use Killing Blows when at medium range from opponents, so that Neo is not left vulnerable to attack.

ZONE MAP

THROUGH THE FLAMES

Exit Ogami's chamber and continue down the passage and around the corner. Additional Assassins move in to attack as the structure begins to collapse in flames. Defeat your opponents, and then Wall Run along the plane to the right past the burning debris.

Defeat the samurai who smash through the sliding doors on either side of the corridor. Before heading outside, smash the furniture in the room to the left to obtain two **Health Packs**, and collect all of the Katana in the opposite chamber. These supplies should prepare you well enough for the challenges lying outdoors.

TAKE IT UP A NOTCH

Cross the bridge to the central area and attack the three samurai standing beneath the gateway. These Assassins are a bit tougher than the ones fought inside, especially the one wearing white. Additional, weaker foes drop from the structure overhead when the enemy in white garb is eliminated.

Cross the frozen water and attack the three Assassins seated around the campfire. Try to knock the enemies into the flames for extra damage, but avoid falling into the fire alongside them.

DEMON NINJA

CLASS:

TRAINING PROGRAM

SPECIAL ABILITIES:

TELEPORTATION

Multi-Opponent tactics are the key to victory here. With a Katana equipped, use Focus to successfully attack one of the three Ninjas, and then press the Special Attack Button to begin a combo attack. If another Ninja is in close enough range, he becomes highlighted with a yellow marker below his feet. Tilt the Movement Control toward him and press Special Attack to engage a multi-opponent sword strike. Meanwhile, use Evade to avoid stun. If Neo's health drops low, avoid staying in the center of the circle. Try to dodge to the outside and attack inward. Continue trying to link up multi-opponent combos on more than one Ninja, and continue this strategy until victory is imminent.

AERIAL TRAINING

"'Hey, Mikey, I think he likes it!' How 'bout some more?"

— Tank

OPPONENTS

Axe Gang Member

Axe Gang Member

AVAILABLE WEAPONS

Axe Gang Axe

Bo Staff

) points

g programs
ard.

ZONE MAP

FLYING AXES

Amid the third wave, enemies in green jackets begin to appear. These enemies are capable of throwing axes. They tend to linger near the corners of the stage, flinging hatchets at Neo. Head for the outer areas and defeat these enemies before the other type. They also drop Axe Gang Axes when taken down.

Use axes to hack through the surrounding throngs of Gang Members more swiftly, building up your score like never before. Target green-suited enemies in the corners and take them out by throwing an axe their way.

NO TIME TO GET DRUNK

Depending on the difficulty level selected, Neo has a specified amount of time to score enough points to complete the level. Failure to score enough points before the time limit expires results in training failure and a do-over. Score points by fighting armed opponents with hand-to-hand and melee weapon techniques. A 300 point bonus is awarded for each full wave defeated.

MODE	POINTS REQUIRED
EASY	5000 PTS.
NORMAL	6000 PTS.
HARD	7000 PTS.

Focus on Multi-Opponent link up techniques, and launch combos against opponents near windows to send them crashing out of the tavern to an instant death. After defeating the first wave, avoid heading downstairs. The trauma to the building structure causes the stairs to collapse. This makes it harder to reach the upper level, where the Operator eventually places a **Bo Staff**.

AERIAL TRAINING

UPPER LEVEL STAFF

After defeating the third wave, the Operator inserts a Bo Staff on the upper level. To reach the upper level, try a Wall Run from the top of the remaining stairs. Or, jump toward the wall beside the stairs, and then press the Jump Button again on contact with the wall. With a little Movement Control guidance, Neo should spring from the wall and onto the upper level.

A staff is the ultimate multi-opponent melee weapon, and it knocks these Gang Members into submission almost instantaneously. When surrounded, tilt the Movement Control toward a different opponent before each Strike to build up the group links. Then, sweeping staff moves become available that allow Neo to defeat all enemies at once! The Bo Staff should help Neo exceed the required score with no problems at all.

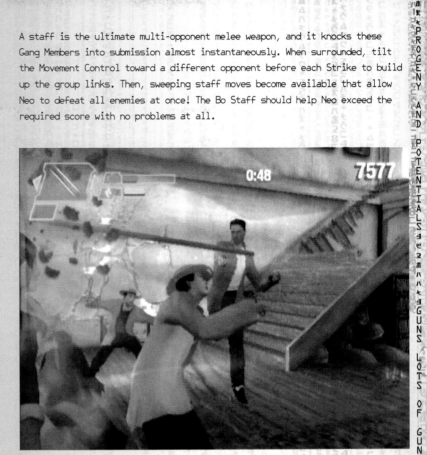

OBJECTIVES

Defeat the Gunrunners Gang.

- Pursue and defeat the Gunrunners' Boss.

Bonus Objective:
- Complete all training programs to unlock a Bonus Award.

WEAPON TRAINING

> "Ten hours straight. He's a machine!"
> - Tank

OPPONENTS

Gunrunner

Gunrunner Boss
(BOSS)

AVAILABLE WEAPONS

Pistol

Heavy Pistol

SMG

STAGE MAP

ZONE MAP

STAKEOUT

Neo's hand-to-hand abilities are disabled by the Operator in order to teach the recruit how to target and shoot. Neo starts the level linked to a low wall on the rear side of the teahouse. Hold the Target Lock Button to make the aiming reticule appear on the enemy in the center of the house. Use the Target Lock controls to quickly switch between targets. When ready step out of hiding and start shooting.

Objectives Updated!

Use Focus to make shots more accurate and close in on enemies while evading fire and shooting. When directly in front of any enemy, hold the Focus Button and press Fire to kick an enemy into the air. Then continue shooting them as they fly to finish them off. If health and ammo run low, dive behind the counter in the corner to find **Health Packs** and a second **Pistol**.

One of the enemies is the Gunrunner Boss. He'll circle the room firing at Neo and then head for the exit. He cannot be hurt at this point, so use Evades to dodge his bullets and stay away from him. When all the other Gunrunners are finished off, chase him toward the exit to continue.

JUMP OUT FROM CORNERS

Head through the corridor after the Gunrunner Boss. After rounding the second corner, a tip appears onscreen regarding corner link-ups. Go ahead and Link-Up with the wall to Neo's right, sidestep over to the corner and peek around. Hold the Target Lock Button to lock onto the Gunrunner lying in ambush, and then press Jump to leap out. Fire while leaping from the corner to catch the Gunrunner off-guard. Link to the corner again and repeat this tactic against other Gunrunners that come running up the long corridor.

When the coast is clear, continue around the next corner and Link Up with the wall. Jump out and kill a Gunrunner, but avoid hitting the cowering civilian with stray bullets.

ZONE MAP

(SAVE CIVILIAN)

(AREA NOT DEPICTED)

AERIAL 360

When Neo reaches the top of a flight of stairs, the Operator contacts him with a kind of hint/warning. Gunrunners lie in ambush out of sight at the bottom of the stairs. Jump from the top of the stairs over the rail. Hold the Target Lock and Focus Buttons while airborne and fire to take out enemies mid-dive.

Pick up a **Health Item** and a **Focus pack** on the mid-level, and then follow the Gunrunner Boss downstairs.

ZONE MAP

ZONE MAP

VIOLENT CONFRONTATION

Link-up with the corner before the next set of stairs. When the Operator is through with his spiel, dive out from the corner and tear up the Gunrunners on the stairs. Wall Run down the staircase to the bottom level, and then press Jump to leap from the wall over the rail. Take out the two guys hiding in the area under the stairs near the **Health Pack**. Meanwhile, the Gunrunner Boss is positioned behind the counter and firing constantly. Avoid his shots as best as possible, and take out all other foes in the area.

DON'T LET HIM GET AWAY!

When all minor enemies in the entryway are dead, the head honcho runs back upstairs. The Operator equips Neo with a couple of SMGs to help clear the road back to the teahouse. Run back upstairs and shoot the boss's two new sidekicks. Perform a Wall Run to get upstairs and get the drop on the two Gunrunners waiting there. Continue following the Gunrunner Boss back to the starting point of the stage.

Unlock "The Code Breaker" Combo!

Fight your way back to the long corridor on the upper level. Notice that the doors on the left side of the passage are now open. Enter this dark space to find the Operator's secret stash. Along with a Health Pack and Focus pack, there is a briefcase that unlocks a Bonus Award combo if you can complete the level.

GUNRUNNER BOSS

CLASS:
TRAINING PROGRAM

SPECIAL ABILITIES:
NONE

Upon returning to the teahouse, Neo finds the area repopulated with enemies. The Gunrunner Boss typically leaps behind the counter by the door and starts firing. Dash to the back of the room and take out all of the other enemies in the area in order to make the Gunrunner Boss vulnerable.

When the Gunrunner Boss's life meter appears onscreen, he's open for business. Link-Up to the backsides of the columns in the room and leap out guns blazing when the boss comes into view. Use Focus to leap into the air and perform Wall Runs, and then soar over the Gunrunner Boss's head while peppering him with lead. Even if Neo is caught out in the open, keep firing and dodging by pressing the Evade Button while strafing left or right. A stationary target is a dead target, or so they say in the gun underground.

DOJO TRAINING

OBJECTIVES

Prove your skill to Morpheus.

Bonus Objective:
Complete all training programs to unlock a Bonus Award.

OPPONENT

Morpheus (BOSS)

AVAILABLE WEAPONS

Bo Staff   Bokken Practice Sword

> "This is a sparring program, similar to the programmed reality of the Matrix. It has the same basic rules. Like gravity. What you must learn is that these rules are no different than those of a computer system. Some of them can be bent. Others can be broken. Understand? Then hit me, if you can."
>
> - Morpheus

STAGE MAP

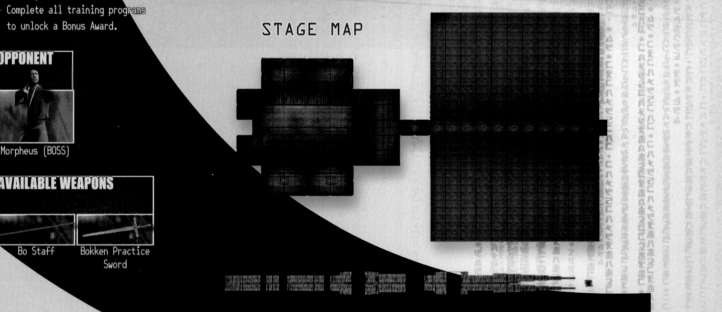

Time for Neo to show Morpheus all that he has learned. The battle takes place in two major stages. At the outset, use Focus to strike Morpheus. Morpheus is very good at dodging subsequent attacks, so triggering combos against him should prove difficult. However, try to avoid Striking at the air too many times, or Neo becomes stunned. Morpheus is just looking for an opportunity to swoop Neo up into the air for a Focus Aerial Throw. In the center of the Dojo, this isn't so bad. But when fighting in one of the side rooms, Neo takes damage both from his hits on the ceiling and the ground.

MORPHEUS

CLASS:

> REBEL

SPECIAL ABILITIES:

> MARTIAL ARTS
> COMBO ATTACKS
> FIREARMS
> MELEE WEAPONS

The best way to get in a long string of Strikes is by using Evade to dodge Morpheus' blows, and then use Focus to attack him from the side or flank. Relish the opportunity to chain together a long string of blows and then finish with a combo, because it will not happen often.

When Morpheus' first health bar is depleted, the battle shifts gears. Neo gets two new skills and a Focus bar extension, but Morpheus is just getting warmed up. The best way to outlast him is to bring weapons into the fray. There are wooden practice weapons situated in the rooms off to the side, in addition to Health Packs and Focus Packs. Grab a Bo Stick or Bokken Sword from a rack and use it to strike and fend off Morpheus, who becomes quite aggressive at this point. Use Focus in combination with Strikes to block Morpheus' moves and counterattack. Morpheus is also likely to pick up a weapon at this point, which means he becomes unable to do his devastating Focus Aerial Throw anymore. As before, do not get too carried away pressing the Strike Button. Press it in succession only after a Strike successfully causes damage, and then try to chain on a few more before attempting a Special Attack and a combo.

ZONE MAP

(WHEW!)

Anyone playing __The Matrix: Path of Neo__ for the first time needs more than one attempt to defeat Morpheus. Just pat yourself on the back for getting through it, and follow Morpheus down the corridor.

RACE TO THE FINISH

In the aerial training, head down the right side of the obstacle course, jumping over the gaps and using Focus while jumping to clear larger gaps. Hold the Focus Button to quickly run up the series of short walls. At the top, jump another gap and then Wall Run on the wall to Neo's right. When Neo stops and curls up near the end, press Jump to leap onto the next platform.

WALL JUMPING EXTREME

Drop to the lower platform and use Focus to clear the extended gaps between platforms. Wall Run and jump again, and use Focus to run up the two low walls. When faced with a higher wall, perform a Wall Run up to the halfway mark as usual, then press Jump to leap higher and grab the ledge. Pull yourself up, and repeat this operation again.

The only way to reach the top of the next area is with Focus Jumps. Start off by collecting the **Focus Pack**, if needed, and then run for the back wall. Use Focus to run up the wall as high as possible and then press Jump and tilt the Movement Control toward the wall to the left or right, whichever is closest. Continue holding Focus as Neo lands and perches on the wall momentarily. Tilt the Movement Control back toward the previous wall and press Jump again. Keep jumping back and forth at an isosceles angle until Neo reaches the top.

Grab the final Focus Pack and head for the end of the platform if Morpheus has a slight lead on Neo at this point, use Focus to try and close the gap. Hold Focus and jump to the final platform where the hard-line is located.

Unlock Character Concepts Page 1!

For completion of all Training levels, the first page of Character Concepts sketches opens in the Media Viewer!

THE WACHOWSKI BROTHERS' VISION

The Operator runs Neo through various melee and skill sims -- a built-in tutorial that primes the player with skills that will be used in ensuing levels.

As the player completes each of the following programs they are awarded RPG upgrades relative to their performance.

Kung Fu Training: Defeat the paramilitary force in the depths of his underground base. Basic hand to hand combat and multi-fighting is introduced.

Sword Training: The player fights the swordsman amongst the swaying bamboo forest.

Winter Training: Follow the path of the tragic samurai in an epic battle against his own assassins' guild that crashes through shoji screen after shoji screen outside into an idyllic Japanese winter.

Aerial Training: The player takes on a gang in the split-level Chinese cafe. This sim focuses on weapons, acrobatics and multi-fighting.

Weapons Training: Take on gunrunners in the tea house. The player focuses on gunplay, acrobatics and multi-fighting.

Dojo: When the player finishes their basic training we segue to the dojo where Morpheus waits until he can be defeated. He is the hardest opponent faced thus far and the player must incorporate a variety of complex acrobatic maneuvers and fight combos to win.

Another segue brings the player to the jump program. Again the gamepath turns from the films in a game of follow the leader across a cut-and-paste skyline of the world's most famous buildings; the Sears Tower, Empire State building, Transamerica building, Tuntex Sky Tower, Menara Telekom, Burj Al Arab, and Petronas Towers. The program ends with a precarious landing atop a perilously high version of the Eiffel Tower.

FILM FOOTAGE

The Lafayette. The Oracle. A betrayal. A sacrifice.

SHINY'S COMMENTARY

Apart from the surprise ending, we were probably most excited by the training missions, and how they were laid out.

Neo could say, "I know kung fu," and the player would get to see exactly how he learned it.

Many games have a tutorial that's almost an afterthought. Instead, we would have several training levels that fit right into the film story that everyone loved.

The jump program level was a difficult cut made early in the development process. It was a memorable moment from the first film, and the Wachowski Brothers' vision of famous buildings made it a tantalizing prospect.

If we're doing another Matrix game, the jump program has to be a part of it.

"Enhanced physical effects
should be evident here with plenty of 'power powder' and 'break-away' environments."

DEJA VU: "IT'S A TRAP!"

> "A déjà vu is usually a glitch in the Matrix. It happens when they change something."
> - Trinity

OBJECTIVES

Reach the wet wall.

OPPONENTS

Police

SWAT

SWAT Captain

AVAILABLE WEAPONS

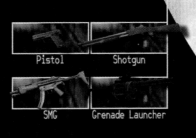

Pistol

Shotgun

SMG

Grenade Launcher

STAGE MAP

STAGE MAP

ZONE MAP

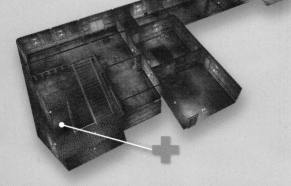

THESE WALLS BETWEEN US

Neo is separated from the rebels by a strange wall that appears from nowhere. Morpheus shouts an instruction to the player – find the building's wet wall so the team can escape. Turn to Neo's left and examine the wall to notice a large crack, from which light emits. Strike the wall to break through into a small room. Neo's Focus meter increases and he obtains the Weapon Strip ability.

Smash through the next wall and use Focus to get the drop on two Police officers in the room. Unlike officers previously encountered, these System denizens have orders to shoot on site. Return fire while approaching all officers, then engage them in hand to hand and disarm them as soon as possible. After Neo's extensive and challenging training, taking down the Police should be an easy matter.

ZONE MAP

BREAKING THROUGH

Open the door into the corridor and rush toward the Police to Neo's left. As they open fire, another mysterious wall appears, cutting off Neo's route. While facing the newly erected wall, turn to Neo's right to spot a fissure. Smash through it into a small bathroom.

Head through two doors back to the corridor on the other side of the new wall and take down the three Police officers. Then go through the double doors in the corridor.

ENVIRONMENTAL EXPLOSIVES

Take down the officers in the storage room, and then look for a crack in the wall in the corner where a **Health Pack** is located. Smash through the wall and immediately use Focus and a pistol to take out a nearby Police officer. There are several exploding environmental objects that can be used to eliminate Police officers in this corridor. Target objects such as wall-mounted fire extinguishers and standing gas cylinders by holding the Focus Button and using the Target Lock controls to switch targets from enemies to explosive

objects. This should severely reduce the number of attacks required to kill the numerous officers in this dangerous passage. Neo gains the 5-Hit Strike Combo and extends his Focus meter as a result of clearing this corridor.

At the far end of the curving passage, shoot the exploding gas cylinder to open a hole in the wall to the room beyond. Make sure Neo is far enough away from the blast to avoid damage.

ZONE MAP

Smash through the final wall to encounter a large Police squad at the top of the stairwell, which is depicted in the very first Zone Map above the section titled "These Walls Between Us" above. Use dual Pistols to return fire on the Police until Neo is in close range, then dive into the crowd and work on striking Neo's multi-opponents combos. After defeating the Police, recharge Neo by heading to the bottom level and collecting the **Health Pack** beneath the stairs. Then return to the middle level of the staircase and go through the archway to the first floor.

BATHROOM RENOVATIONS

Continue forcing open doors and smashing through cracked walls and head through a series of bathrooms, taking down any Police encountered along the way.

ZONE MAPS

NAVIGATING THE MAZE

Head up the passage and around the corner to the right. Neo is again cut off from weapons and supplies by a mysterious wall. Go through the double doors and shoot the fire extinguisher and/or gas cylinder to kill the Police inside. Head through the next two bathrooms, eliminating additional Police. Continue through the double doors and take down the trio guarding a **Health Pack** near the Matrix-created wall. Break through a fissure in the wall opposite Neo's entry point to continue.

HEAVIER FIREPOWER

Continue fighting through the next room and into the corridor. Head to Neo's right and around the corner to encounter a SWAT team. These guys are armed with **Submachine Guns (SMGs)**, so be sure to use Focus to evade bullets and Link-Up to the backside of the support column on the left wall of the  corridor for cover while returning fire. Approach and engage the SWAT with hand-to-hand combat, and all of the enemies soon stop firing their weapons. After Neo takes down the SWAT unit and moves beyond the mid-point of the passage, another mysterious wall appears. Neo has no choice but to go forward.

STAIRWAY ASSAULT

Head around the corner to Neo's left, only to be sealed in by another wall. Move to the wall near the archway leading to the stairs and Link-up to the wall. Stay in this position until a SWAT unit appears, and the point man walks through the arch. Step out and use Special Attack on him from behind for a Silent Takedown.

Quickly enter the stairwell thereafter and use hand-to-hand to take down the tougher, more dangerous SWAT Captain. The morale of all SWAT oficers in the area drops when the SWAT Captain is eliminated. However, SWAT Captains are tougher enemies, with greater weapons and hand-to-hand fighting abilities.

Descend the stairs to the bottom level to recover with a **Health Pack**, and then go up to the top level. Collect the **Focus Pack** in the corner, and then smash through the cracked wall to the right.

ZONE MAP

APOC STEPS UP

Collect a **Health Pack** and **Shotgun** in the room, and then approach the door in the corner. As the sound of voices in the next corridor indicates, another SWAT unit lies in ambush. After slamming through the door, use Focus and fire down the corridor, being careful to avoid an exploding fire extinguisher on Neo's left.

Head down the passage a few steps until Apoc suddenly joins the fray. Help Apoc take down the SWAT unit and their captain, and then follow Apoc through the double doors.

Apoc blocks the last door until Neo goes to the corner and obtains the **Grenade Launcher**. While standing near the Grenade Launcher, press the Weapon Swap Button to exchange Neo's Pistols for the launcher, and then follow Apoc into the next room where Morpheus and the rest of the gang wait.

HOLD ONTO THE LAUNCHER

As Apoc suggests, the launcher should be extremely useful against enemies in the next stage. Be sure to hold onto it, and do not swap it for any weapons or Detonation Packs in the next level.

The Path of Neo

Master Abilities become unlocked on the second ring of the Path of Neo. In addition to the 5-Hit Combo obtained during the previous stage, the player has a choice between two new upgrades. The two choices available now include Weapon Strip Level 2 and Off Wall Strike Level 2 that improves the ability gained during the Dojo Training level. To view an upgrade in action, highlight it with the cursor and press the displayed Select Button to bring up a menu. Choose "View this upgrade" and watch a short animation of the growth move in action. View both upgrades to determine how Neo's fighting abilities should improve. The player *must* choose an upgrade before the next level can be initiated.

THE WACHOWSKI BROTHERS' VISION

The player must battle through the dragnet of swarming s.w.a.t. troops and escape.

Though Trinity, Apoc and Switch are more than combat capable, the player will be relied upon to protect their backs, fleeing through the cavernous basement of the Lafayette hotel and the vast sewer system beneath the city.

FILM FOOTAGE

Cypher. "Not like this." "Yes." "No!" "Guns. Lots of guns."

SHINY'S COMMENTARY

It's funny to think that we've gone through a few hours of gameplay already, and we're really just getting started.

We really wanted to focus on Neo as the ship's "rookie" - at this point in the movie, everyone has a gun except Neo, and he only gets one when Apoc hands him his backup pistol. And that's exactly where you start the level.

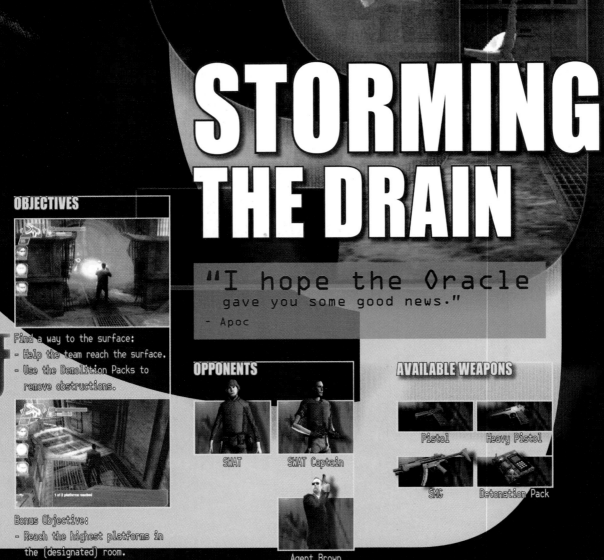

STORMING THE DRAIN

"I hope the Oracle gave you some good news."
- Apoc

OBJECTIVES

Find a way to the surface:
- Help the team reach the surface.
- Use the Demolition Packs to remove obstructions.

1 of 2 platforms reached

Bonus Objective:
- Reach the highest platforms in the (designated) room.

OPPONENTS

SWAT

SWAT Captain

Agent Brown

AVAILABLE WEAPONS

Pistol

Heavy Pistol

SMG

Detonation Pack

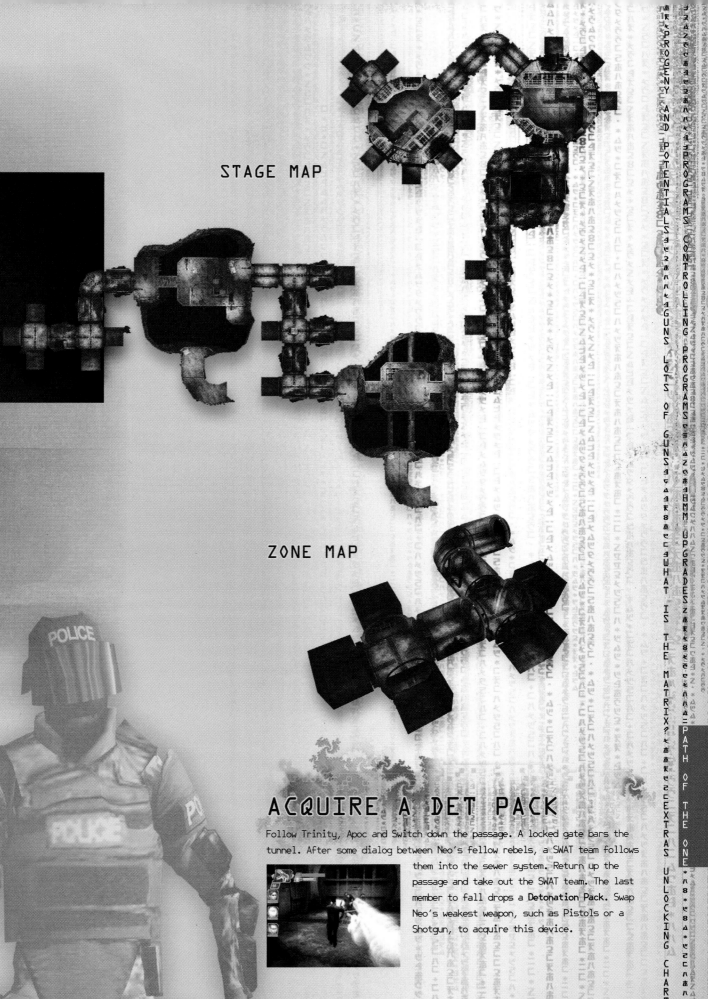

STAGE MAP

ZONE MAP

ACQUIRE A DET PACK

Follow Trinity, Apoc and Switch down the passage. A locked gate bars the tunnel. After some dialog between Neo's fellow rebels, a SWAT team follows them into the sewer system. Return up the passage and take out the SWAT team. The last member to fall drops a **Detonation Pack.** Swap Neo's weakest weapon, such as Pistols or a Shotgun, to acquire this device.

GET THE DROP ON RAPPELLING SWAT

When SWAT units are rapelling down manholes or out of helicopters, they are unaware of Neo's position on the ground. Gain the advantage by running up behind rappelling SWAT unit members as they descend. Press the Special Attack Button to snap a SWAT member's neck before he even has time to draw a weapon!

ZONE MAP

BLOW THE GATE

Return to the gate with the Detonation Pack selected in Neo's weapon window. Press the Fire Button to set and arm the Det Pack near the gate. The remote trigger icon then appears in Neo's weapon window. Move a safe distance away, taking cover behind a tunnel support, and then press Fire again to detonate the charges and destroy the gate.

ZONE MAP

UNEXPECTED HELP

Use Focus to reach the far end of the corridor quickly, where a SWAT team rappels down from the level above. Either that, or take them all out instantaneously with a grenade fired from the Grenade Launcher at medium range. Disarm and disable the remainder of the team, and then hide behind a nearby support column. Another SWAT unit in the next passage sets charges on the nearby gate and detonates them, opening the way for Neo and the rebels to proceed.

Head through the destroyed gate, firing SMGs on the SWAT unit at the far end of the passage. When you've taken them down, head around the corner.

REMOVING STRUCTURAL SUPPORTS

Proceed onto the suspended platform and take out the SWAT members that rappel from above. One of the men drops another **Detonation Pack**. Place this device near the lone support column in the center of the platform. Then head back toward the stairs where Trinity, Apoc and Switch stand before blowing the charges. The upper platform collapses in the blast, dropping the SWAT team members in addition to a **Health Pack**. Head up the blast-forged "ramp" to the upper level where a **Focus Pack** lies. Continue through the sewers.

ZONE MAP

HANGING AROUND WITH BROWN

Neo must survive against Agent Brown for several moments. At this stage, Neo is unable to defeat an Agent. Brown usually initiates battle by firing at Neo. Return fire with a Grenade Launcher to knock Brown off his feet. Then approach within close distance to engage Brown in hand-to-hand, and try to stay near enough to the Agent that he does not draw his pistol again.

The idea here is to kill time until Trinity and the others can create an escape path for Neo by blasting through the rock wall erected by the Matrix. Avoid striking Brown unless he moves in to attack himself. Brown has a tendency to remain in idle combat stance without attacking, as if to him this were a "standoff". Go ahead and let him think that, and leave him standing there idle as long as he likes. Use Evade to back-flip away from Brown's strikes, especially if Neo is stunned.

CHANGE IN PLANS

If a SWAT team member in the previous passage dropped a Det Pack, then set it near the central support column. If not, then move down onto the platform and continue taking out SWAT units that drop around Neo until one of them drops a **Detonation Pack**.

Set the Det Pack near the center column and move back toward Trinity and the others. However, *do not set off the Det Pack!* A change in the Matrix eliminates the stairs, trapping Neo on the bottom level. Quickly cycle through available weapons, just so the Det Pack remote is no longer Neo's equipped weapon. While Trinity and the others try to find a way to set off the charges themselves, an Agent drops to the platform and attacks!

Dodge to the side of Brown when he lunges, and use Focus to attack him from the side or behind. If you can manage to drive him to the edge of the

platform, use Focus + Evade to back-flip away and blast him with the Grenade Launcher. This should knock him off the platform for a temporary death. Brown soon returns to the platform, taunting Neo. However, this seemingly useless action still buys Neo time until the others blast through the cave wall.

LEAP TO ESCAPE!

Keep an eye on the bottom of the screen while dancing with Brown. When Trinity and the others manage to blast through the cave wall, a tip appears at the bottom of the screen regarding long jumps. Head toward the point where the stairs used to exist, hold Focus and press Jump to clear the gap. Afterward, turn around and perform another Focus Jump to return to the platform. Follow Trinity and the others to the upper level, collecting the **Health Pack** and **Detonation Pack** lying near the edge of the next tunnel sector.

PROCEEDING AND IMPROVING

Set the Det Pack on the next gate barring the path, and stand back before blowing the charges. Proceed through the gate and halfway down the passage to encounter another SWAT team. Take them all out with a well-placed grenade, if still available. Neo gains the Focus Aerial Throw ability for defeating this unit. Continue defeating SWAT units and collecting Detonation Packs, then use them to blow the next gate obstructing the rebels' escape path.

ZONE MAP

ZONE MAP

PROVIDE COVER FIRE

Blow the final gate with a Det Pack, and then proceed into a multi-level room. SWAT rappel down on the opposite platform, and into the room below. As Trinity orders, stay on the first platform and shoot at the SWAT on the opposite platform. When the accompanying trio gets to the opposite platform, they can take down the SWAT at close range. Drop into the room below and take down the one guy who rappelled all the way to the bottom. Use either ladder to climb back up to the mid-level.

Objectives Updated

Unlock Quick Kicks Combo!

In the first multi-level chamber near the end of the stage, look to Neo's right just after entering the room. A series of platforms allows Neo to reach the two platforms located high above the room. You can tell Neo is standing on the right platform when the camera automatically sweeps out to a wide angle. Mastery of Wall Running and Wall Jumping is required. Jump onto the platform to the right of the entrance, then Wall Run from there over to the next-highest platform. From there, Wall Run straight up the wall and then Wall Jump over to the platform on the left side of your screen. Touching the platform triggers a conrmation message.

Drop to the platform just below the balcony, then Wall Run continuously from platform to platform, over the entrance and beyond. After the last platform, there is a long stretch of wall. Wall Run along the wall as far as possible, then Wall Jump before falling to reach the second platform. Touching both platforms in this chamber unlocks the Quick Kicks Combo. All you have to do at this point is complete the level to obtain the new move. Heavy Pistols and Grenade Launchers are also located on the top level.

2 of 2 platforms reached

ZONE MAP

SURFACING

The rebels emerge in another multi-level room. Drop into the chamber below and take out the SWAT team. Then climb the ladder up to where Trinity and the others wait, and take the final ladder to the surface.

LOBBY SHOOTING SPREE

OBJECTIVES

Locate and rescue Morpheus:

- Infiltrate the Government Building and terminate all enemies.
- Trinity is your partner. Work together. Protect her.
- Destroy the elevator shaft and gain access to the roof.

"Morpheus believed something, and he was ready to give his life for what he believed. I understand that now. That's why I have to go, because I believe in something. I believe I can bring him back."

- Neo

OPPONENTS

AVAILABLE WEAPONS

SWAT

SWAT Captain (BOSS)

Riot Police (BOSS)

Pistol

Heavy Pistol

SMG

Shotgun

Tear Gas Grenades

Fragmentation Grenades

ZONE MAP

RELIVING INFAMY

Neo and Trinity enter the Government Building with guns - *lots* of guns - to rescue Morpheus. In the lobby, they must face off against several waves of heavily armed SWAT and Riot Police units. When the action commences, use an Evade roll to reach the columns on the side of the room. Target and fire on enemies while racing up the side of the room behind the columns. Approach enemies with guns drawn and use Focus to boot them into the air; continue pumping them with bullets as they fly. Use Weapon Strip and hand-to-hand to disarm and defeat the SWAT unit.

GRENADES ARE YOUR BUDDIES!

At least one member of the first wave should drop Tear Gas Grenades. Be sure to pick these up, swapping them for Neo's Pistols if you have to, since they are so extremely useful against subsequent SWAT waves.

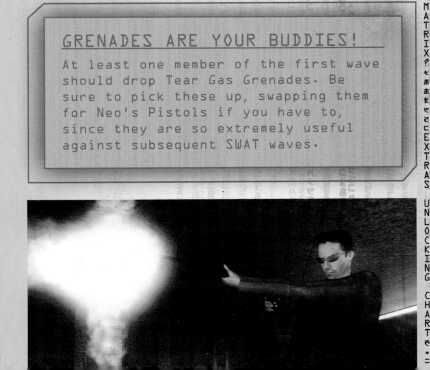

SWAT CAPTAIN

CLASS:

SWAT

SPECIAL ABILITIES:

NONE

A SWAT Captain of greater strength, stamina and combat ability accompanies the second wave. Therefore, he must be taken down first, but not at the risk of leaving Trinity to fight all of the other SWAT units. That would be like hanging her out to dry. As soon as the second wave is loaded and action commences, charge forward using Focus and lob a Tear Gas Grenade at the group.

While the SWAT team chokes and wheezes, unable to attack, find the SWAT Captain amid the chaos and kick his teeth in. He is usually located in the center of the area near the elevator, and wears green instead of black and no helmet. Fire on him while approaching, then close the distance and use Focus plus strikes and combos to drive his health bar down as quickly as possible. If Neo kicks the Captain away before he's finished, fire upon him again while closing the distance, then attack. When the Captain crumples into the corner like a rag doll, assist Trinity in taking down the rest of the SWAT. One of the team should drop Fragmentation Grenades. Equip these at the cost of Pistols or Shotguns in preparation for the next wave.

The final wave is the smallest, but toughest. Two SWAT guys, a SWAT Captain, and three Riot Police whose life gauges appear onscreen. The strategy that makes this battle one of the easiest fights in the game is to charge forward immediately, using Focus and ignoring any damage to Neo. When two-thirds of the way across the lobby, target the center group of Riot Police and toss a Fragmentation Grenade. With sharp timing, at least two if not all of the Riot Police can be taken down instantly. Take out the remainders by using incessant Strikes to make them drop their shields, and then riddle the remaining foes with bullets. The SWAT Captain in the last group is not a boss as in the previous wave, but he does supply a morale boost to the other men while around. Single out and eliminate him immediately after the Riot Police, and then clean up the remainders.

RIOT POLICE TRIO

CLASS:	
	RIOT POLICE

SPECIAL ABILITIES:	
	SHIELD BASH

THIRTY SECONDS UNTIL CRITICAL

When the last government agent drops lifeless to the floor, Morpheus' critical meter in the upper right corner of the screen starts going crazy. 30 seconds remain until you must reach the elevator at the top of the lobby. Use Focus if needed to slow time, especially if Neo is positioned at the opposite end of the lobby following the battle.

The Path of Neo

Two new abilities become available in Neo's upgrade menu: Tornado Throw in the first ring and Off Wall Super Level 2 in the second ring. Choose an ability before moving on.

FILM FOOTAGE

Neo saves Morpheus. Neo saves Trinity. "They're not out yet." "Mr. Anderson!" "He's beginning to believe."

SHINY'S COMMENTARY

The Lobby served as a focal point during the early stages of development. Just about everything we did on the game, we did in this level first.

It was a proving ground for most of the game's systems, a demo level at E3, and a test level for focus groups.

At this stage in Neo's growth, he still shouldn't be able to take on Agents by himself and survive (for very long at least), so the teamwork mechanic with you dodging bullets and Trinity shooting the Agent worked well in this level.

THE WACHOWSKI BROTHERS' VISION

As Trinity and Neo are on a timetable in the film, a "Morpheus clock" will be incorporated through each section of the government building level. If it expires before each sublevel is completed, so does Zion and so do you.

The lobby fight will remain fairly true to the film. Vanquish the guards and soldiers before the "Morpheus clock" expires. The player will again be relied upon to protect Trinity as well.

After a film insert of Trinity and Neo arming the bomb in the elevator and riding the counterweights up the shaft, the game action resumes as the player leaves behind the burning elevator shaft and fights their way though a bevy of military types as they ascend a Mario Bros.-like construction of ladders and metal staircases that weave through the building's enormous heating and cooling systems.

When at last the player accesses the roof and dispatches the final soldiers there, they must stay alive in any way possible until Trinity can get into position and kill Agent Jones.

The final section of gameplay takes place in the helicopter. This sequence needs to be a hyperbolized version of the scene in the film. The player circles the government building clearing the rooms and adjoining rooms of the Agents and soldiers, while avoiding pursuing police helicopters. When the final agent is killed before time expires, Morpheus will break his bonds and run.

ROOFTOP ASSAULT: "DODGE THIS"

> "Let me tell you what I believe. I believe Morpheus means more to me than he does to you. I believe if you are really serious about saving him you are going to need my help. And since I am the ranking officer on this ship if you don't like it, I believe you can go to hell. Because you aren't going anywhere else."
>
> - Trinity

OBJECTIVES

Locate and rescue Morpheus:
- Trinity is your partner. Work together. Protect her.
- Use Bullet Dodge to defeat Agent Jones.

- Shoot down the helicopter to stop the troops.

OPPONENTS

SWAT

SWAT Captain

Riot Police

Agent Jones
(BOSS)

AVAILABLE WEAPONS

Pistol

Heavy Pistol

Assault Rifle

SHOCKING RESULTS!

Toss enemies into one of the two large electric generators on top of the building, on either side of the entrance door. Shocking volts of electricity course through the enemy's body, usually killing them. Just avoid touching the generator yourself, or Neo may be in for a bit of a shock himself. Also use exploding environmental objects such as fire extinguishers and fan motors to take out SWAT, Riot Police and Agent Jones.

CLASSIC MOVES

When Agent Jones appears on top of the Government Building, Neo immediately learns the Bullet Dodge ability. As Agent Jones commences firing on Neo, hold the Focus Button and hold the Evade Button to perform Neo's trademark move. While Neo is avoiding flying bullets, Trinity runs in from the side and executes

Jones. Use this tactic to eliminate Jones whenever the Agent possesses another enemy. If Jones engages Trinity in combat, draw his attention by shooting him. Bullet Dodge only works when Neo is completely still and not in a hand-to-hand fighting stance.

INCOMING!

Soon after Jones' demise, a helicopter flies overhead and drops off more SWAT. Charge at them and eliminate them as quickly as possible, before Jones has a chance to possess one of them and return to the battle. Remember that Neo can swiftly eliminate rappelling enemies by attacking them from behind just after they land. If Jones cannot possess a member of a wave, he drops from the helicopter between waves. This is easier than trying to take him out during a wave.

SHOOT DOWN THAT CHOPPER!

Acquire an Assault Rifle from one of the SWAT enemies by any means necessary. After the helicopter drops off a few waves of law enforcement, Trinity orders Neo to take down the chopper. At this point, a life gauge for the chopper appears onscreen, as though it were a boss. Fire on the chopper each subsequent time it appears and drops off SWAT, using Focus to steady Neo's aim and improve accuracy.

TAKE DOWN CAPTAINS!

SWAT Captains drop onto the rooftop with certain waves, boosting morale and carrying Grenade Launchers. Defeat these enemies swiftly if Agent Jones is not around. Use the Grenade Launcher to take out clusters of enemies and to fend off Agent Jones, as long as Trinity is not in range of the blast.

OPERATOR HERE:
Eliminate the Riot Police!

Riot Police use Flash-Bang Grenades to blind Neo and Trinity. If one of these goes off, the screen fills with white for up to five seconds. This is a missed window of opportunity you cannot afford. Take down Riot Police quickly, either by knocking them off the roof or by attacking them from behind. To get behind a Riot officer, use Focus and Evade to position Neo behind them and attack them from the rear to them drop their shields instantly.

LEAP OF FAITH

While Trinity hijacks a helicopter, Neo acquires the Double Jump ability. Just then, Jones and a new cadre of SWAT storm the rooftop. Morpheus' situation again turns critical, leaving Neo just thirty seconds to get off the rooftop. Run toward the helicopter, using Focus to avoid bullets and reduce the enemies' ability to fire. Jump onto the skylight, then hold Focus and leap toward the helicopter. Continue holding Focus as Neo rises, and press the Jump Button a second time at the full height of his jump to reach the chopper.

OBJECTIVES

Locate and rescue Morpheus:
- Defeat all Soldiers.

- Defeat all Agents.

Bonus Objective:
- Destroy the enemy helicopter
- Unlock bonus material.

HELICOPTER RESCUE

OPPONENTS

SWAT   Agent Jones

Agent Brown   Agent Smith

"Morpheus believes in you, Neo.
And no one, not you, not even me, can convince him otherwise. He believes it so blindly that he's going to sacrifice his life to save yours. You're going to have to make a choice. In the one hand you'll have Morpheus' life, and in the other hand you'll have your own. One of you is going to die. Which one will be up to you."

- The Oracle

STRAFING THE ROOF

Neo mans the helicopter's chain gun against the remaining forces in the building. Use the Movement Control to swivel the gattling gun, and press the Focus Button for accurate aiming. Continue holding the Focus Button until each enemy is hit. The Gatling gun is extremely powerful, and only two or three bullets kill an enemy. During this mission Neo regains some Focus for each enemy killed. Avoid wasting Focus energy by only using it to hone your aim and shoot.

STAGE MAP

Once Trinity narrows down Morpheus' location, she makes a final swing around the rooftop. All of the remaining enemies must be killed. Clean up quickly by shooting the crane cable to drop the cargo box on top of several SWAT at once. On the next pass, shoot the base of the crane itself to take out more troopers as well as the rooftop entrance.

"BRING THAT BUILDING DOWN!"

When SWAT and an agent appear in a nearby building, Trinity swings around so that Neo can take them out. There's too much cover for the enemies to hide in, so shoot the support column in the center of the building to collapse the entire structure.

BUILDING SIDES

Trinity then descends to the side of the building, where SWAT and an Agent offer resistance. Avoid overheating the chain gun by shooting only in bursts. If the chain gun begins to glow red, lay off the Fire Button for a full second to let her cool down.

INCOMING MISSILES

Trinity then swings out to the side of the building only to encounter the enemy helicopter once again. Use Focus and Fire to spray the chopper with bullets. When it launches a guided missile at your chopper, aim for the missile to destroy it before it strikes and causes damage to Neo.

HELICOPTER INTERFERENCE

After Neo eliminates all the soldiers on the building corner, Trinity swings around to face a helicopter. Press and hold both the Focus and Fire Buttons and really let the helicopter have it! Although it is doubtful that the helicopter can be eliminated in a single pass, it is important to bring that bird down in order to avoid being attacked later and to unlock a special bonus.

Let the Gatling gun cool for a brief second as Trinity swings around. When the enemy helicopter comes back into sight, combine Focus with an extended barrage to finally bring it down. This is the last encounter with the helicopter, so make it count!

After the chopper hovers near the building a few seconds, specially trained SWAT officers with missile launchers fire from the upper level. First shoot down the rockets to avoid damage to the chopper or Neo, and then take out the guys on the upper level.

Unlock Art Graveyard!

Shoot down the enemy helicopter during this stage to unlock the Art Graveyard page in the Media Viewer. This section contains screenshots and concept art designs of levels that were expunged from the game.

When Trinity moves the chopper in closer to the room where Morpheus sits, keep an eye on the doorway to the left. Blast the Agents when they attempt to reenter the room. Morpheus finally breaks free of his chains and leaps for the chopper.

RESCUE MORPHEUS

At last, Trinity swings around to the room where Morpheus is being held. Shoot through the glass on the center level to hit the Agents on either side of Morpheus. Watch that you do not shoot directly into the center of the area, because hitting Morpheus means mission failure.

SUBWAY SHOWDOWN

OBJECTIVES

Defeat Agent Smith.

Find a way out.

OPPONENT

Agent Smith
(BOSS)

STAGE MAP

ZONE MAP

"I'm going
to enjoy watching
you die, Mr.
Anderson."
- Smith

AGENT SMITH

CLASS:
AGENT

SPECIAL ABILITIES:
BULLET DODGE
FIST BOUQUET

The classic confrontation has arrived! If you would like to start off the battle the same way Neo and Smith did in the film, then run toward the column on Neo's left. Use Focus to start a Wall Run off the column, then push the Special Attack Button with the right timing to start an Off Wall Super. Continue holding Focus, target Smith and start shooting. If you empty Neo's Pistol, Smith and Neo reenact the classic dialog that followed that scene from the film.

Now down to business. Use Strikes to block Agent Smith's attacks, then use Focus to counterattack. Neo still does not have the ability to kill an Agent such as Smith. Try to drive Smith onto the train tracks, and keep him there until a train passes by. If Smith is run over on the tracks, the train kills him. However, if Smith is aware of the train approaching, he quickly disengages from combat and leaps out of harm's way.

Therefore, you must knock Smith onto the tracks and render him into a stun or prone state in the instant just before a train passes. Basically, this battle could take a while. The longer it takes to throw Smith under the train, the bigger the drain should be on Neo's health and Focus. If you need to recover, use the Health Pack located on the other side of the phone booth. Focus can only be recovered by sparring with Smith in real time.

ZONE MAP

ZONE MAP

GOING DEEPER

Neo gains the Aerial Killing Blow ability after defeating Agent Smith. However, the Agent quickly returns and knocks Neo through a station wall. Now you must find an alternate route out of the station.

Head around the corner and down the hall. Go through the doorway on Neo's left to hear a rumbling noise and a few muffled threats from Smith. Then go through the door on the opposite side of the corridor. Continue down the corridor until Neo crashes through the floor and drops a level.

Turn around and head down the passage. Smith possesses the homeless man behind the bars, so quickly slide down the slope to avoid taking fire. Ascend the steps and proceed down the passage until Neo notices something is wrong with the Matrix.

The Path of Neo

The Atman Principles become available in the fourth ring of the Path. Some of these upgrades are permanent, some only last through the next level. The one Atman Principle available is Heal Others, which allows Neo to heal allies in a short radius. This skill can only be used once, and only remains in effect until Neo swaps it for another weapon or clears the next level. As for more permanent upgrades, Aerial Strike Level 2 and Off Wall Super Level 2 are now available on the second ring of the path. Choose one of these three upgrades to proceed to the next level.

THE WACHOWSKI BROTHERS' VISION

This should be a good long boss fight. Incorporating the speeding trains into the battle will give the player different opportunities to defeat Smith.

After a brief transition the player will begin a long chase through the teeming markets and tenements of the urban sprawl, until they reach the "heart o' the city" hotel.

If the player opts to fight the Agents during the chase defeating more than one at a time should be close to impossible.

FILM FOOTAGE

Neo dies. Neo lives. "He is the one."

SHINY'S COMMENTARY

The Wachowski Brothers initially called it a "brief transition," but we collaborated on a large underground level that explored themes that were first introduced in segments of the Animatrix, where areas of the Matrix are breaking down and starting to malfunction. The "haunted train" level came out of those discussions.

STUCK IN THE LOOP

OBJECTIVES

Find a way out of the train station:
- Find a token for the train.

- Get to the phone at the back of the train.

- Stop the train when it reaches the Balboa Station.

"The Matrix is a system, Neo. That system is our enemy. But when you're inside, look around, what do you see? Businessmen, teachers, lawyers, carpenters. The very minds of the people we are trying to save. But until we do, these people are still a part of that system, and that makes them our enemy. You have to understand most of these people are not ready to be unplugged. And many of them are so inert so hopelessly dependent on the system that they will fight to protect it."

- Morpheus

OPPONENTS

SWAT

Soldier

Soldier, Heavy Weapons

Agent Smith

AVAILABLE WEAPONS

Heavy Pistol

Assault Rifle

SMG

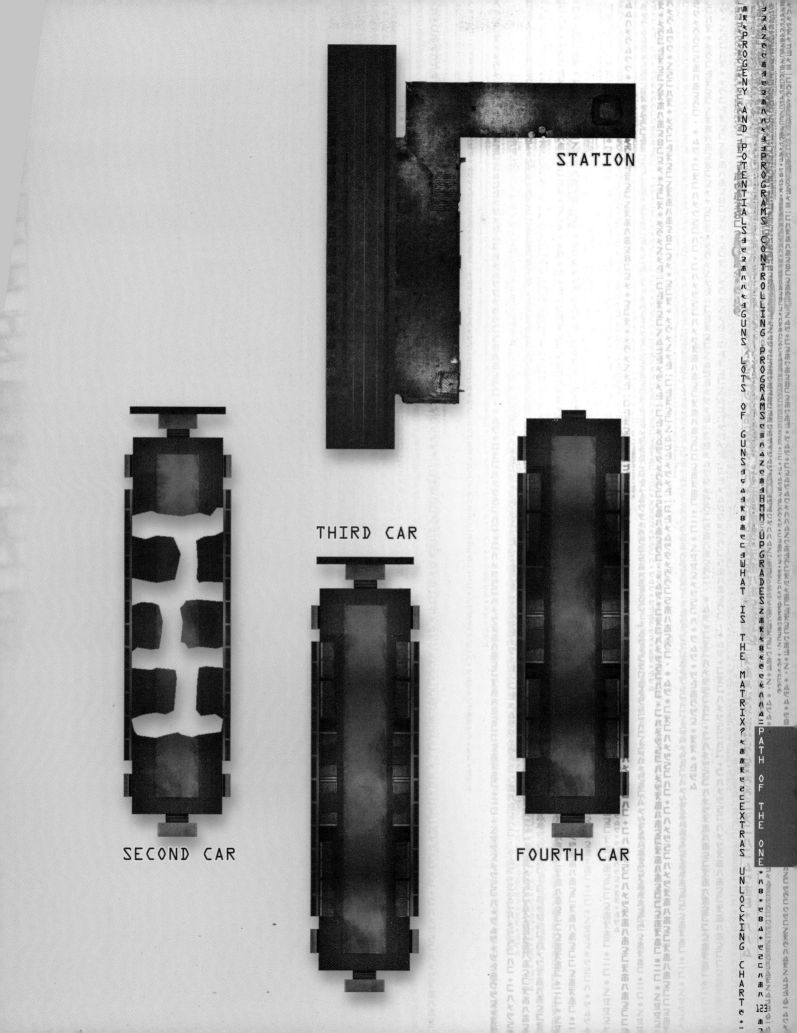

STATION

THIRD CAR

SECOND CAR

FOURTH CAR

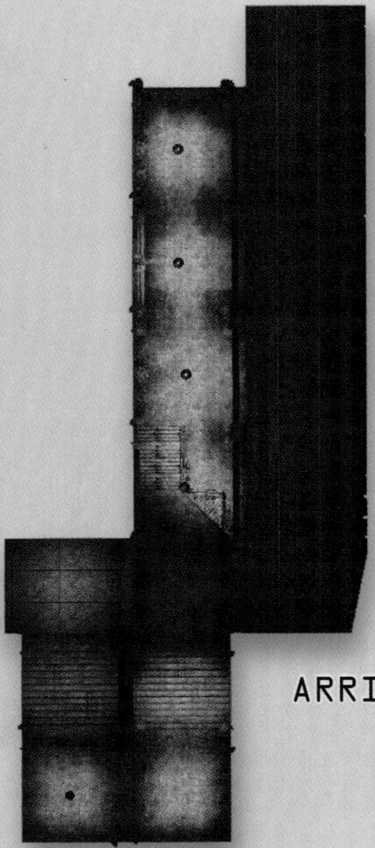

ARRIVAL

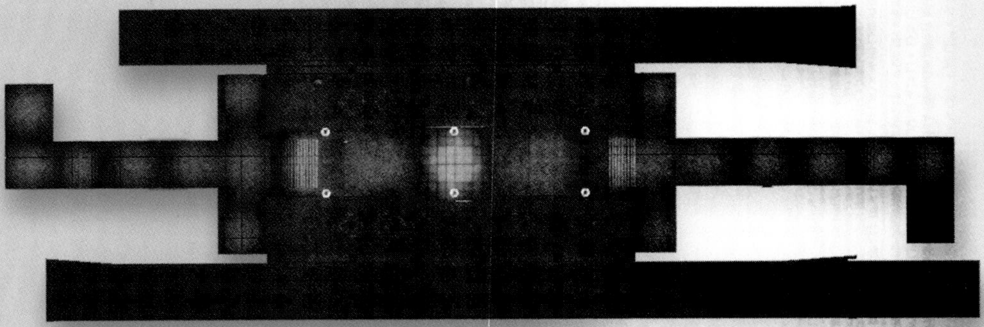

TOKEN

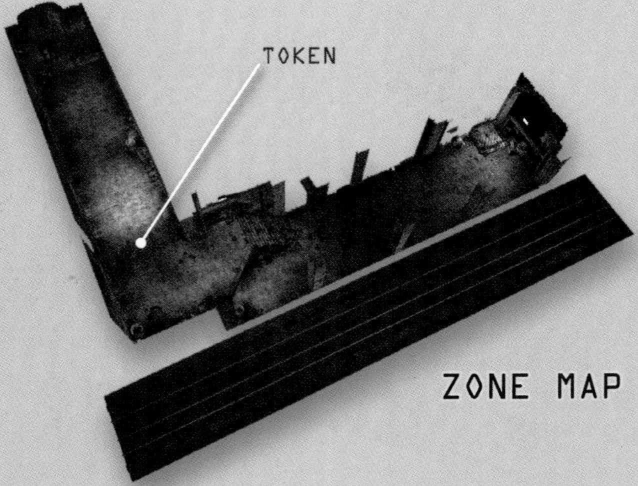

ZONE MAP

PLATFORM

Approach the conductor to trigger a conversation, then head to the back of the car and go through the door. The train is suddenly moving, but the train car is turned on its side! Proceed past the floating passengers and proceed to the next car.

Objectives Updated

Jump on the visible platforms before they disappear to cross the train car. Head through the door to the final car. The trick in to reaching the phone is to use Focus when running. Otherwise, the car continues to stretch out, preventing Neo from reaching the phone. When the button icon appears onscreen, press the Action Button to pick up the phone and dial the Operator.

BROKEN RULES

Proceed out to the train platform and wait for the train to arrive. The conductor instructs Neo to go and get a token. Head back to the turnstiles and press the Action Button grab one of the tokens floating in the air. Return to the conductor, press Action to hand over the token, and board the train.

ROTATING THE CAR

Return to the train car that was previously turned on its side. This time, the car should be completely upside down. Exit the door you came through, and then return to find the car on its other side. Exit and return one more time to finally find the train car right side up.

Position Neo in front of the glowing red button on the left side of the train car at the opposite end. Wait until the next time the conductor announces Balboa Station, and then immediately press the Action Button to stop the train. If the conductor does not seem to be announcing it, move away from the switch and immediately run back.

ZONE MAP

ZONE MAP

BACK WHERE THE MATRIX MAKES SENSE

At the arrival destination, quickly head up the stairs and take down a trio of armed SWAT to obtain their SMGs. Open the door and head through the double doors on Neo's left.

After a call to the Operator, Neo learns that he's fallen into a trap. The Operator tries to describe a possible way out, but is cut off--something about jumping onto a flatbed train.

SUBJECT OF DERISION

Neo encounters Smith again, this time accompanied by a crack team of Soldiers. Move over to the columns and take out the Soldiers firing from the cover of structural supports. Continue moving around the station, taking down more Soldiers as needed. When Smith attacks, do your best to avoid him. Smith cannot be defeated during this level, but he can be removed momentarily by throwing him in front of a passing train.

After fighting waves of Soldiers and fending off Smith for a while, industrial trains start moving down the tracks on one side of the station in place of subways. Move over to that side of the station and evade attacks until a flatbed car appears. Leap onto the flatbed to be carried to an exit point. Climb the ladder to escape from the station.

THE CHASE: "I NEED AN EXIT!"

"Mr. Wizard, get me the hell out of here!"
- Neo

OBJECTIVE

Flee from the Agents!

OPPONENTS

Agent Brown

Agent Jones

Agent Smith

AVAILABLE WEAPON

Heavy Pistol

STAGE MAP

ZONE MAP

I SEE POSSESSED PEOPLE

Race around the corner of the garbage truck to get out of Smith's line of fire, and continue down the block to the left. Head straight through the market area to the back corner. Weave in and out of the fruit stands to make the Agents' shots miss. Locate the **Health Pack** and the **Briefcase** behind the corner fruit stands. After collecting the case, be sure to survive to the end of the level in order to unlock a secret.

ZONE MAP

HE IS THE ONE

"Neo, I'm not afraid anymore.
The Oracle told me that I'd fall in love, and that
the man that I loved would be the One. So you see,
you can't be dead. You can't be. Because I love you.
You hear me? I love you. Now, get up."

- Trinity

OBJECTIVES

Defeat the Agents.

OPPONENTS

Police   Agent Brown (BOSS)

Agent Jones (BOSS)   Agent Smith (BOSS)

AVAILABLE WEAPONS

Pistol   Heavy Pistol

STAGE MAP

ZONE MAP

Neo immediately learns the Bullet Stop ability. Hold the Focus and Evade Buttons to stop the Agents' bullets just shy of hitting Neo. Then press the Fire Button when the icon appears onscreen to send the projectiles flying back. The Agents dodge the bullets of course, but this at least gives Neo an opportunity to get the jump on hand-to-hand combat.

Neo now has the ability to defeat Agents hand-to-hand. While fighting, Agents whose health has grown low will possess Police and civilians in the rooms surrounding the hallway. Take out Police officers before the Agents can possess them, reducing the number of "lives" each Agent can use.

Fight the Agents by using Strikes to block their attacks. Then use Focus to counterattack. Attempt to fight all of the Agents at once and trigger Multi-Opponent Combos. Once Neo staggers an Agent, use a Special Attack to knock them off balance and trigger a devastating combo.

Continue fighting the Agents until all are defeated. Agent Smith returns to the scene for one last solo match. Match blows with him and show him what a little Focus can do. Agent Smith is the last obstacle that stands in Neo's way to becoming the One. Do not let up now!

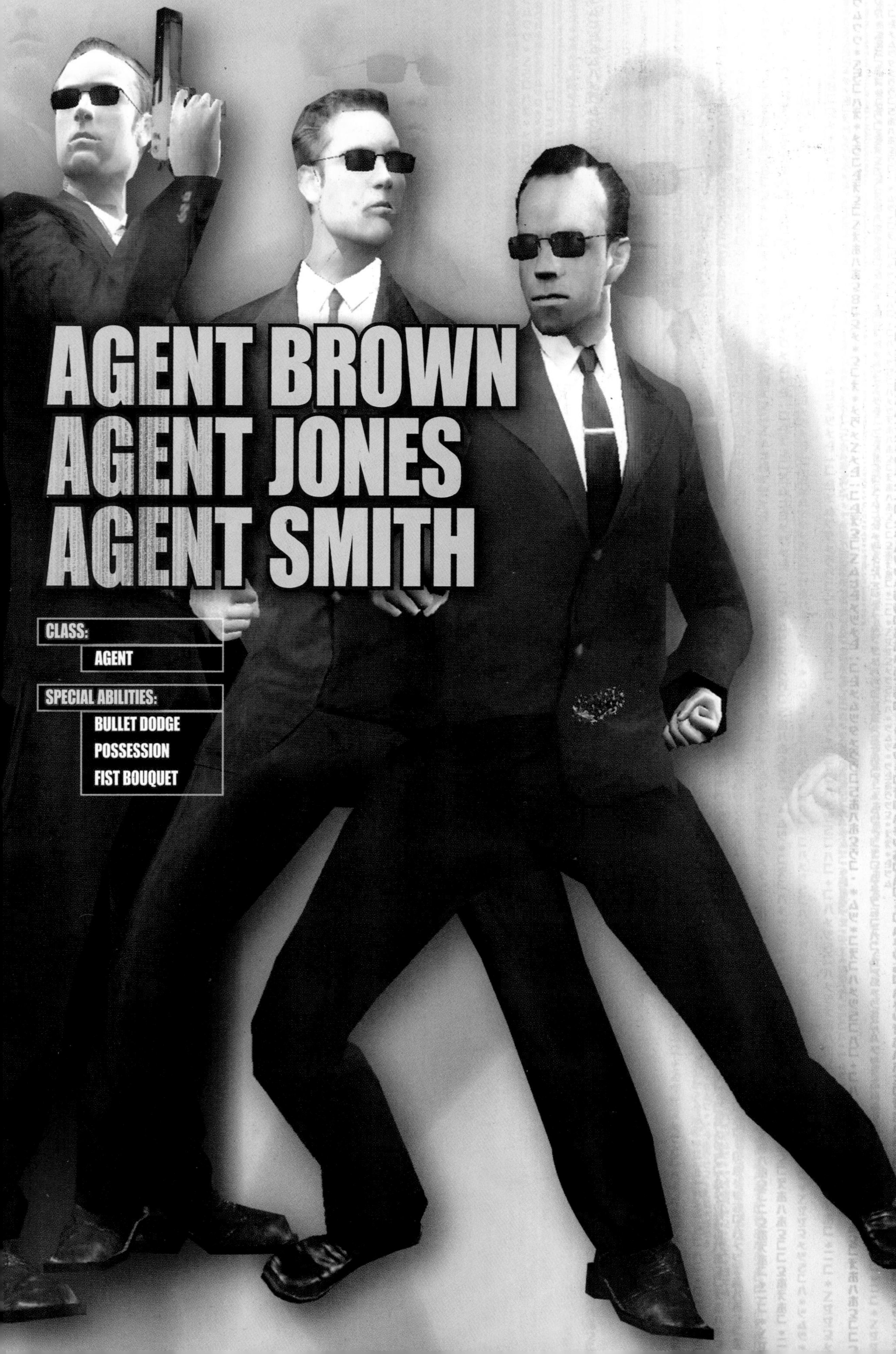

AGENT BROWN
AGENT JONES
AGENT SMITH

CLASS:
AGENT

SPECIAL ABILITIES:
BULLET DODGE
POSSESSION
FIST BOUQUET

The Path of Neo

Although Neo has finally stepped up to become the One, not much is new on the upgrade scene. Killing Blow Level 2 is now available on the second ring, and the Revive skill is available for temporary attainment on the Atman Principles outer ring.

THE WACHOWSKI BROTHERS' VISION

(Aware of the complexities of the buggy camera issues when dealing with a hallway fight, we would like to re-investigate incorporating this scene into the gamepath. Utilizing "invisible" walls or stylistically dissolving the structure away to matrix code transparencies, might offer a solution.)

Before the player begins gameplay, they will be given additional skills to upgrade as well as a generous amount of RPG points to spend. They are then pitted against the three Agents until Smith is defeated.

FILM FOOTAGE

As Neo flies away, the bird's eye view reveals itself to be an image on the bank of monitors in the Architect's office. The image suddenly snap-zooms back to the street intersection where a lone figure stares up among the flow of walking dead pedestrians; the kid. The Architect calls for his general. "The end has begun."

HE IS THE ONE

REDPILL RESCUE: THE HEALER

OBJECTIVES

Find the Redpill.

Defend the Redpill.

Get the Redpill out safely.

"Consider what we have seen, Councilor. Consider that in the past six months, we have freed more minds than in six years."
— Morpheus

OPPONENTS

Soldier   SWAT

AVAILABLE WEAPONS

Heavy Pistol   Sawed-Off Shotgun

SMG

STAGE MAP

NEO: THE ONE

Now that he is the One, Neo must attempt to rescue potential rebels targeted by the System because they have seen something wrong with the Matrix. Known as "Redpills", these individuals must be unplugged before Agents and other servants of the Machines can get to them.

The stage begins as Neo soars high above the city, doing his "Superman-thang." Five city blocks are illuminated below. Use the Movement Control to highlight one of the city areas, and press the Select Button to attempt a Redpill rescue. The civilians can be rescued in any order.

In all of these missions, Neo must defeat all of the enemies encountered in the level and prevent the Redpills from being killed during the action.

ZONE MAP

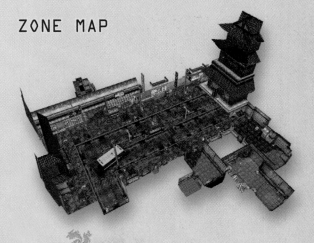

CHINATOWN STREET WAR

Proceed out of the alleyway into the street and talk to the two civilians. As indicated, the Healer's shop is across the street. Follow the central passage to a doorway bearing a sign that reads "Red Pill Herbal Remedies." Obvious enough for you?

After meeting the Healer, head out of the store and defeat the newly arrived SWAT team in the street. After Neo takes out the first wave, a Chinatown gang emerges from one of the nearby clubs to help Neo protect the Healer. Head down the street and shoot the SWAT officers perched on the overhead ledge. Take down the SWAT Captain who emerges from Neo's starting point.

Return to the herbal shop to find the Healer, and lead him down the street toward Neo's starting point. The Healer moves slowly. Still, follow him and take out additional SWAT appearing on the street and in the alley.

Neo and the Healer find that a change has occurred in the Matrix, cutting off Neo's exit. The Healer starts to return to his shop. Head back into the street ahead of the Healer and defeat all of the new enemies. Follow the Healer back to his shop, where he unlocks and opens the backdoor.

ZONE MAP

WAREHOUSE INVASION

In the warehouse behind the Healer's shop, a SWAT unit smashes through the overhead windows and rappels into the room. Remember to eliminate at least one enemy with a Silent Takedown, by sneaking up behind them as they land and use the Special Attack Button. Shoot and beat up the rest of the SWAT unit, and then follow the Healer to the warehouse exit door.

Checkpoint saved

TUSSLE UNDER THE TRACKS

Stay near the Healer as he moves down the street. In this area, enemies will target and shoot the Healer to prevent him from going with Neo. Shoot SWAT officers that jump out of green doors on either side of the street, and shield the Healer from harm with your own body if necessary. Continue protecting the

Healer up to the corner, where Neo encounters a huge SWAT team accompanied by a SWAT Captain and Soldiers. Take out all the enemies while the Healer remains at the corner. If Neo's health drops to fifty percent or less, move near the Healer and he will replenish Neo's lost life.

As soon as the street is clear, Agent Brown appears and attacks Neo and the Healer. Take him out with Focus attacks, and do your best to keep him from

the Healer. If allowed to get close enough, Brown will not hesitate to walk right up to the old man and start shooting him in the head. Taking out Agents should be no problem for Neo, now that he is the One.

The Path of Neo

After rescuing The Healer, Atman Principles ring to di the Jackpot temporary abili available. This Atman Princ the place of one of Neo's w and can be used by pressing Button. The effect raises N Focus, Health and Focus reg rates, and damage output fo attacks. Jackpot lasts for minutes, and can only be us

REDPILL RESCUE: THE LIBRARIAN

"Only human."
- Agent Jones

OBJECTIVES

Defend the Redpill.

OPPONENTS

Soldier

Agent Brown

Agent Jones

AVAILABLE WEAPONS

Heavy Pistol

SMG

Flash-Bang Grenades

STAGE MAP

A BOOK OUT OF PLACE

Fight Agents Brown and Jones until the Librarian reaches the top level of the Library. Quickly jump up to her level, and continue fighting the Agents until the Librarian finally exits to momentary safety. Any time the Librarian is in danger and prevented from advancing, her onscreen health icon pulsates with red light.

ZONE MAP

ZONE MAP

PICKING UP THE CLUTTER

Follow the Librarian through the corridor and into the reading room, collecting a **Health Pack** along the way. While the Librarian hurries ahead, take out the Soldiers who rappel down into the hall. Find a box of **Flash-Bang Grenades** in the corner, and then head through the door to the right of the one Neo entered.

ZONE MAPS

MAIN HALL BRAWL

Collect the **Health Pack** near the desk, and then climb up the ladder to the loft. The Librarian falls out the window, but the level below is just a short drop. Jump through the window and into the Main Hall.

Defeat the waves of soldiers that burst into the room. The Soldiers do not attack the Librarian, so there are no worries there. Defeat the Soldiers in standard order, and then prepare for a final battle against Agent Jones. Unlike the soldiers, Jones does indeed attack the Librarian if he gets close enough to her.

The Path of Neo

Rescuing the Librarian enables the Focus 360 Clear Out ability--the Master Ability. Hold Focus, press Strike and Special Attack simultaneously, and then rotate the Movement Control in a circle. Neo draws up a small amount of energy and slams his fist into the ground, creating a ripple wave effect that knocks all enemies backward, possibly stunning them.

REDPILL RESCUE: THE SECURITY GUARD

OBJECTIVES

Rescue the Security Guard.

Bonus Objective:
- Defeat five enemies within 30 seconds.

"There is some fiction in your truth, and some truth in your fiction. To know the truth, you must risk everything."
- Anonymous

OPPONENTS

Riot Police

SWAT

SWAT Captain

Agent White (BOSS)

AVAILABLE WEAPONS

Heavy Pistol

Shotgun

Flash-Bang Grenades

SMG

Fragmentation Grenades

STAGE MAP

CHURCH TOWER 1F

CHURCH TOWER 3F

CHURCH TOWER 2F

CHURCH TOWER 4F

143

ASCENSION

Follow the Security Guard up the stairs, taking out SWAT unit officers along the way. There are some **Fragmentation Grenades** on the landing where the first SWAT team shows up so be certain to obtain them.

In the upper levels, a stairway crumbles under Neo. Try to land on the level directly below, rather than dropping all the way to the bottom of the tower. Afterward, Neo gains the Antigravity Jump. This allows him to clear the gap by performing a Focus Jump.

BELL
TOWER
STAIRS

SIDE CHALLENGE

Can you eliminate the SWAT Captain and Riot Police on the uppermost balcony in extremely short order? If you procured some Fragmentation Grenades, then the answer is yes. Use Focus to slow time and Wall Run along the wall by the stairs leading up to the floor where the tactical unit is perched. At around the mid-point of the stairs, lob a grenade at the enemy group. Challenge complete!

Unlock Hyper Strike Combo!

Defeat the enemy set on the uppermost level of the staircase area within the given timeframe. The surest method to completion is to use Fragmentation Grenades dropped by SWAT enemies. Then complete the level to unlock the Hyper Strike Combo, viewable in the Extras Menu. The number of enemies and the time allotment changes depending on the choice of difficulty level, so there may be some variance in Easy and Hard modes.

BELL TOWER

Smith's replacement in the Matrix's trio of supernatural enforcers has taken it upon himself to deprive Neo the satisfaction of rescuing the Security Guard. At first, Neo must fight Agent White mano-a-mano. Strike to block his attacks, use Focus Evade moves to spin to White's flank, and attack him from the side or rear with Focus combo moves. Build up strikes and then launch into a combo. Repeat this action until White's first incarnation is defeated.

White reappears, this time pointing his gun at the Security Guard's head. Attack White before he finishes speaking and shoots the Security Guard. A SWAT team storms the bell tower as White and Neo fight. When his health is low, White attempts to possess another SWAT team member somewhere in the belfry. After the SWAT team appears, move around the tower while fighting White and use SMGs or Shotgun blasts to eliminate the SWAT team. Use Focus to target and shoot the large wooden beams supporting the bells above the SWAT units. When the beams collapse, the bells fall and crush the men below. This reduces Agent White's number of available 'lives.' However, keep in mind that protecting the Security Guard is top priority. Do not become so engaged with the SWAT units that White is allowed to kill the Security Guard.

AGENT WHITE

CLASS:
AGENT

SPECIAL ABILITIES:
BULLET DODGE
POSSESSION
FIST BOUQUET

The Path of Neo

Clearing the Security Guard rescue mission unlocks the Spoon ability on the Path of Neo screen. Be sure to view the upgrade, as the animation is quite amusing! This upgrade does not affect Neo's abilities in any manner. Instead, acquiring this unlocks the Zion Archives stage on the Level Select screen. This level contains discarded character models from stages of the game that failed to make the cut.

REDPILL RESCUE: SKULL'S LAMENT

OBJECTIVES

Find the Redpill.

Defend the Redpill.

OPPONENTS

SWAT

SWAT Captain

Chuang Tzu (BOSS)

Agent Brown (BOSS)

Agent Jones (BOSS)

AVAILABLE WEAPONS

Heavy Pistol

Sawed-Off Shotgun

SMG

Assault Rifle

Fragmentation Grenades

Detonation Pack

STAGE MAP

STOPPING THE RAID

A SWAT team is positioned and ready outside Chuang Tzu's loft, only their backs are all turned when Neo enters. Walk quietly up behind one of the SWAT team members at the back of the formation and use a Focused Silent Takedown to eliminate him. Take out the rest of the SWAT team, and be sure to collect their weapons and some Fragmentation Grenades.

Work your way down to the SWAT Captains positioned near Chuang Tzu's door and take them out as well. Another SWAT team emerges from the elevator. Use Focus to target and shoot fire extinguishers and other exploding objects near the corridor walls surrounding the second SWAT team to cut down their numbers.

CHUANG TZU

CLASS:

REDPILL

SPECIAL ABILITIES:

MARTIAL ARTS

Chuang Tzu challenges Neo to a fight. Although this is merely a contest to earn respect, do not go lightly on this talented Redpill. His blocking speed and strength of attack are surprisingly high. He already performs many Focus attacks and combos, in spite of the fact that he is still 'plugged in.' Chuang Tzu uses Focus jumps to leap over Neo's head, stunning him, and then performs a Super Jump attack to knock Neo down. But Neo's Focus ability sets him just above Chuang Tzu in that respect. Use Focus Strikes and combos to attack Chuang Tzu, and do not let up until he relents. Once you start a combo, extend the combo and cause as much damage to Chuang Tzu, without allowing him to get a punch in edgewise. If Chuang Tzu manages to leap up to one of the lofts, run under the platform so that he cannot drop from above to stun and attack Neo. Defeating Chuang Tzu earns Neo a longer Focus meter and the 6-Hit Strike Combo ability.

FULL BREACH

SWAT officers crash through all of Chuang Tzu's windows. Luckily, the previous battle settled all of Chuang Tzu's questions about Neo, and he is now ready to fight side-by-side with the One. Take out the officers with extreme prejudice, throwing Fragmentation Grenades at SWAT in the corners of the room. Just make sure that Chuang Tzu is not standing in the blast radius, since grenades can certainly wipe him out.

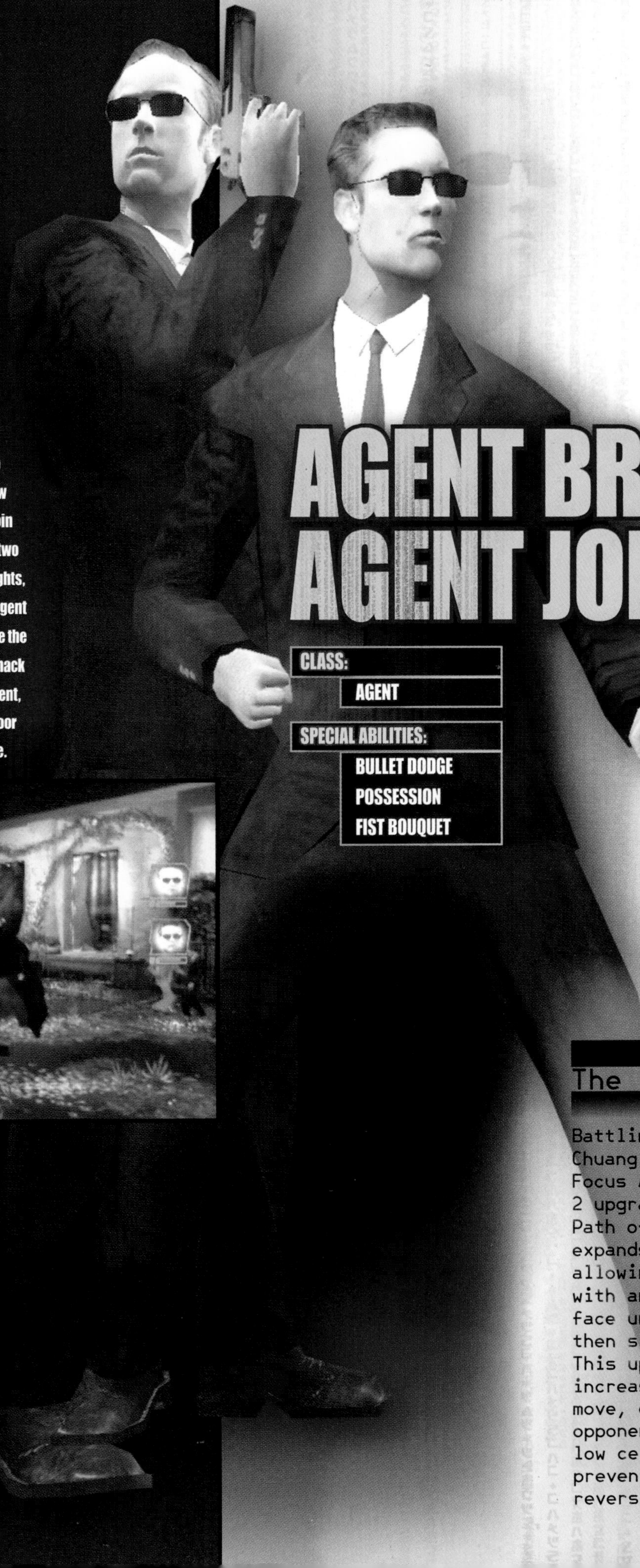

Agents Brown and Jones leap through the windows, ready to murder Chuang Tzu rather than allow him to unplug from the System. Join Chuang Tzu in the battle against the two Agents. Fight whichever one he fights, using Focus attacks to clobber the Agent from behind. This will not discourage the other Agent from trying to bushwhack Neo. But by double-teaming an Agent, Neo and Chuang Tzu can wipe the floor with them, one pencil-neck at a time.

AGENT BROWN, AGENT JONES

CLASS:
    AGENT

SPECIAL ABILITIES:
    BULLET DODGE
    POSSESSION
    FIST BOUQUET

The Path of Neo

Battling to victory alongside Chuang Tzu unlocks the Focus Aerial Throw Level 2 upgrade on the second Path of Neo. This upgrade expands the original move, allowing Neo to fly upward with an opponent, place his face under Neo's heel, and then slam him to the ground. This upgrade dramatically increases the damage of the move, especially when the opponent is slammed into a low ceiling. Also, Agents are prevented from escaping or reversing the move.

REDPILL RESCUE: THE KEY

OBJECTIVES

Defend the Redpill

OPPONENTS

Doberman

Doberman Boss
(BOSS)

AVAILABLE WEAPONS

Sawed-Off Shotgun   SMG

STAGE MAP

ZONE MAP

151

DOBERMAN BOSS

CLASS:

> DOBERMAN

SPECIAL ABILITIES:

> HYPER EVADE
>
> RAGE

A young potential is being held prisoner in Club Hel, the Merovingian's private nightclub, by Exile programs known as "Dobermen." After Neo introduces himself, lead the girl downstairs to confront her captors. Dobermen are a class of Exile program, with special claw attacks that can stun Neo instantly. Fighting them is a little bit like fighting a less aggressive and less defensive Agent.

The Doberman Boss's life gauge appears onscreen. While he has more stamina than the other Dobermen, he has no special abilities that the others do not. Allow the group to surround Neo, and then use Multi-Opponent Strikes and Combos to level the playing field. When the Doberman boss begins to weaken, concentrate on taking him out of the battle. Use Focus Strikes to build up to a combo, and then unleash the dogs.

Defeating the Doberman Boss will not shake up the underlings nor affect their morale any, since they are not human. After the room is cleared, the doormen from the hallway above may enter the room and attack. If not, look for them in the hallway beyond the VIP lounge. Take the Health Pack behind the bar, if needed.

ZONE MAP

The columns in the dark coat check area provide cover from gunfire. Approach one of the Dobermen and use Weapon Strip to disarm him. Then proceed to kick his teeth in, and use Focus to strike up a combo and finish him off. Due to the close proximity of the columns, moves like Tornado Throw work extremely well (especially when you can whip a Doberman into a column three or four times before flinging him across the room). Use Killing Blow and Aerial Killing Blow to encourage the Dobermen not to be shy.

Unlock Storyboard Sequence 1!

Rescue the Club Kid and complete the level without using a single weapon. Fulfilling this condition unlocks the Storyboard Sequence 1 Extra on the Making Of screen.

ZONE MAP

TIME TO CHECK OUT

Return to the corner where the Club Kid cowers. After she finds her 'magic key', she's ready to leave. Lead her up the passage to the coat check area to face the remainder of the club's bouncers.

THE WACHOWSKI BROTHERS' VISION

In the few months in the narrative between The Matrix and The Matrix Reloaded, Neo saves "...more minds in six months than in six years." This idea will be elaborated on where gameplay will consist of Neo soaring through the city protecting "redpills" from a cadre of pursuing Agents, police and police vehicles.

The player should be able to locate the "redpills" by peering through the veil of coded reality of the city with their "Neo-sight."

Once an attack is joined and stopped, the player will have saved a mind and must hurry to protect the next. The action will become more hectic as multiple "redpill" life bars appear on the HUD as they are under attack. You must save a certain amount to continue but ultimately the more you save, the more "consciousness" points you earn.

FILM FOOTAGE

Neo's nightmare. A gift. "Agents?!"

SHINY'S COMMENTARY

Again, the Animatrix served as an inspiration for many of these levels, as well as the Matrix comics.

Each Redpill has something special that makes them unique, something that has awakened them to the illusion of the Matrix.

We took that concept further, to the point where the Redpills could actually help Neo, whether healing the player or even fighting alongside him.

"This should feel a bit like a
pinball bonus where lots of balls are suddenly released, cascading and ricocheting all over the place."

THE CAPTAINS' MEETING

OBJECTIVES

Cover the Captains' exit from the meeting:
- Defeat the Upgraded Agents.

OPPONENTS

Riot Police

SHAT

Agent Jackson
(BOSS)

Agent Johnson
(BOSS)

Agent Thompson
(BOSS)

AVAILABLE WEAPONS

Heavy Pistol

SMG

ZONE MAP

STAGE MAP

UPGRADED AGENTS

CLASS:	
	AGENT

SPECIAL ABILITIES:	
	BULLET DODGE
	POSSESSION
	FIST BOUQUET

Upgraded Agents are capable of blocking more of Neo's attacks and they regenerate their health automatically yet at a slow rate. Therefore, it is important to keep an eye on the Agents' health gauges and determine when one is weakening. Keep attacking a wounded Agent until he is defeated, thus reducing the number of enemies and improving Neo's survival chances. Remember to use Multi-Opponent combos and moves like Tornado Throw to attack all of the Agents at simultaneously. Use the Health Pack on the upper level of the loading dock if needed to regain life.

ZONE MAP

TIME FOR NEO'S ESCAPE

After defeating the Upgraded Agents, Neo gains the Code Vision ability. Use this newfound skill to look through the walls and see the tactical team about to break through the door. Two Riot Police among the group equipped

with gas masks prove
even more difficult to
disarm than previously
encountered ones. They
can bash Neo more swiftly
and frequently than their
lesser counterparts. Use
Evade moves to get behind
the shielded Soldiers
and Strike from the rear
to make them drop their
shields.

Proceed outside and shoot the SWAT unit officers on the balcony and in front of the van. Take out the remaining enemies to clear the level.

OBJECTIVES

Get to Ballard in the kitchen.

Eliminate opposition in the kitchen.

Get to the freight elevator.

Lead Ballad to the restaurant's front door.

CAPTAINS' RESCUE: RESCUE BALLARD

Neo once again soars high over the city, this time with higher stakes. Following the ambush on the meeting, five of the Captains are in danger of being captured, or even worse, killed. Use the Movement Control to highlight one of the city blocks below, and press the Select button to fly to the rescue. Unlike the Redpill Rescue missions, the path does not continue if Neo fails to rescue a Captain.

OPPONENTS

Soldier

SWAT

Agent Jackson (BOSS)

Soldier, Heavy Weapons

Agent Johnson (BOSS)

Agent Thompson (BOSS)

AVAILABLE WEAPONS

Heavy Pistol

Shotgun

Sawed-Off Shotgun

Assault Rifle

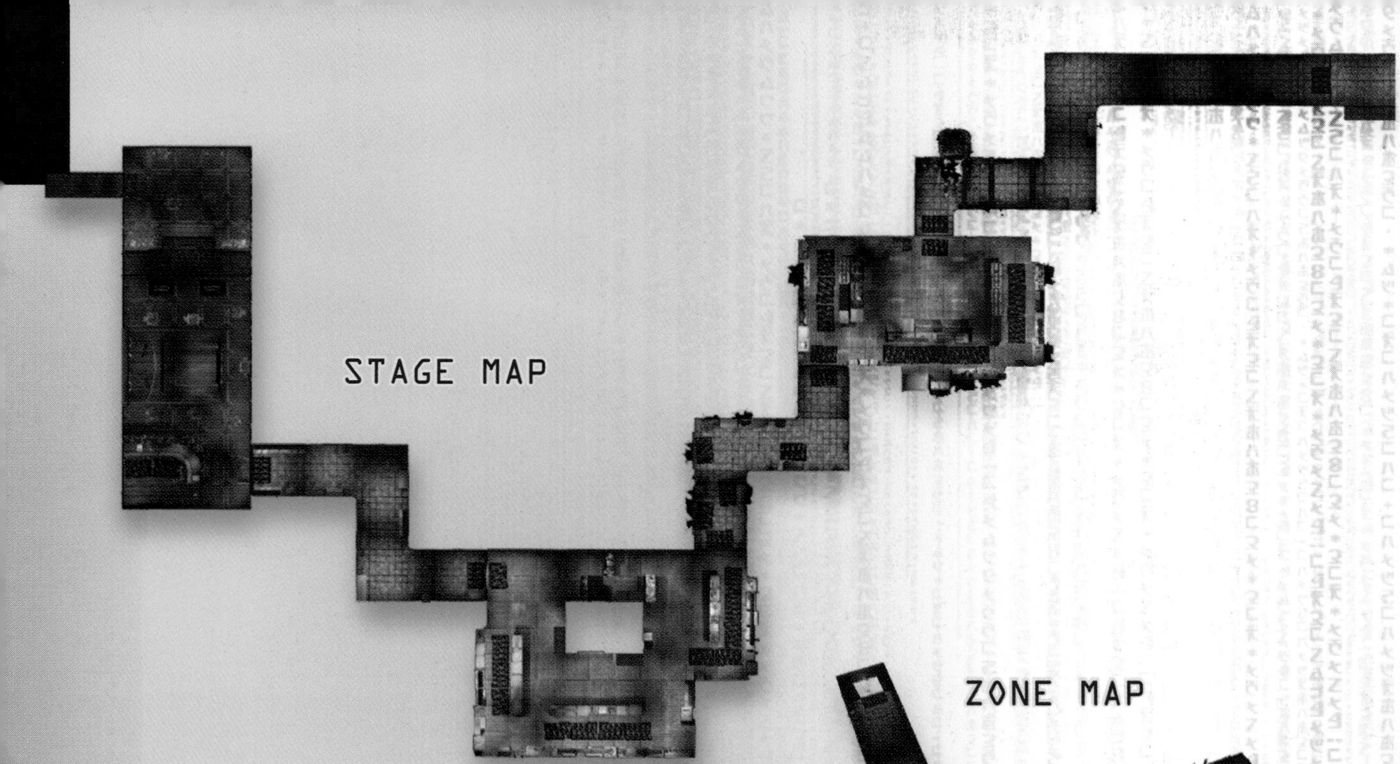

STAGE MAP

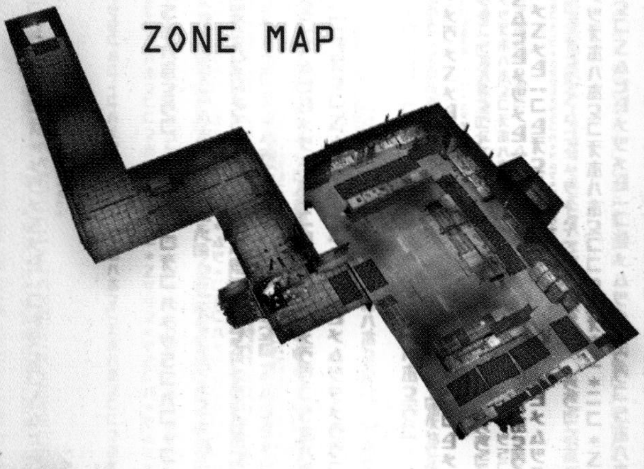

ZONE MAP

THE CALM BEFORE THE WAR

It seems System forces
have cornered Ballard
in the business front
restaurant. Sneak up on
the closest SWAT guy and
eliminate him with a
Weapon Strip. Take out
his buddy, as well as
the third man around the
corner.

TAKE THE KITCHEN

Head into the kitchen and make your way around
the stoves and island counters, blasting SWAT
with a Shotgun. This is a shootout, so make no
mistake about it and eliminate the foes swiftly.
Watch out for exploding gas stoves and fire
extinguishers that are mounted on walls, and try
to make use of these things against the enemies.

FREIGHT ELEVATOR TRAP

When the kitchen is clear, follow Ballard back to the freight elevator. However, avoid getting too close, because the elevator is rigged! Use an Evade move at just the right instant, and it may be possible to avoid harm. Tricky, but possible.

SO NOW WHAT?

Head back through the kitchen and down the corridor into the second kitchen. Continue eliminating the Soldiers with Shotgun blasts, and disarm as many foes as possible with Weapon Strip maneuvers.

BALLARD'S RESCUE

Collect the **Shotguns** and **Health Pack** Ballard stashed behind the bar, and use the counter surface as cover to return fire on the multiple Heavy Weapons Soldiers crowding the room. Another Health Pack lies on the upper level at the back of the dining area, so fight your way through the Soldiers to get to it if needed. When the last soldier drops like a sack of bricks, the Upgraded Agents storm the restaurant.

ZONE MAP

ZONE MAP

With Ballard's help, this should prove even easier. Although Ballard is no match for an Agent, he does tend to distract the foes from attacking Neo. Use this your advantage by attacking any Agent from behind who goes after Ballard. As before, refuse Agents the right to retaliate by blocking their strikes, then use Focus to counterattack. Chain together an extended combo such as Machine Gun kicks or Hyper Strike, and continue slamming your guy around until he unplugs. Team up with Ballard to defeat all three Upgraded Agents to complete the level.

UPGRADED AGENTS

CLASS:

AGENT

SPECIAL ABILITIES:

BULLET DODGE

POSSESSION

FIST BOUQUET

The Path of Neo

The Reflect Bullets Atman Principle becomes a Master Ability on the Path of Neo. When chosen, this ability fills a slot in the weapon cycle. To use the skill, cycle through Neo's weapons until the Reflect Bullets icon is displayed, and then press Fire to activate. All bullets aimed at Neo are automatically reflected back at the enemy who fired, killing them if possible. The ability remains in effect for one minute, and can be used up to three times. Like many Atman Principles, Reflect Bullets is a temporary upgrade that disappears after the next level is cleared.

CAPTAINS' RESCUE: RESCUE NIOBE

OBJECTIVES

Rescue Niobe. Lead her to the exit:
- Lead Niobe to her exit on the top level.

- Shut the doors on the middle levels.

OPPONENTS

SWAT

Agent Jackson (BOSS)

Agent Johnson (BOSS)

Agent Thompson (BOSS)

AVAILABLE WEAPONS

Heavy Pistol

Shotgun

SEWER JUNCTION 1F

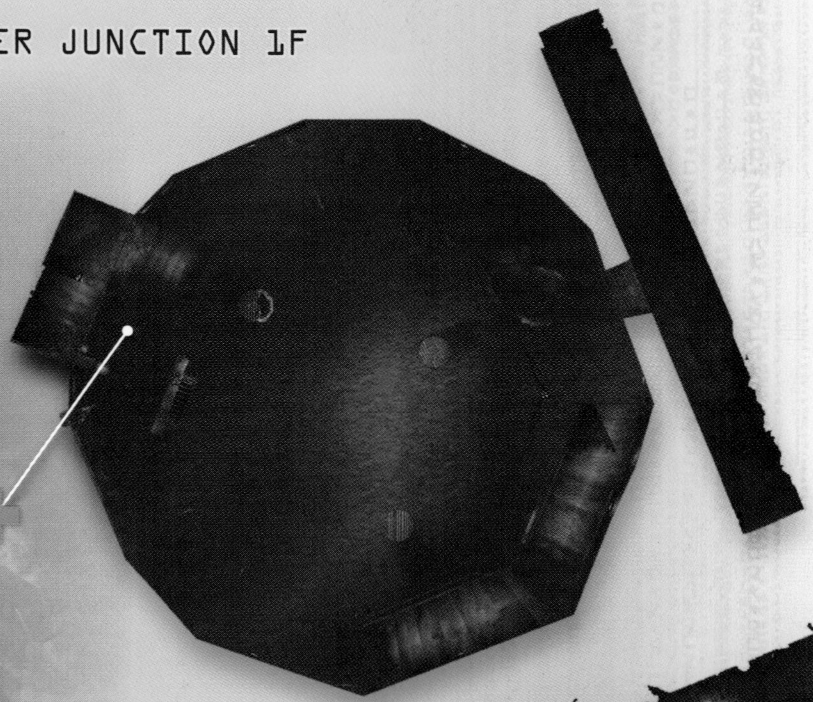

SEWER JUNCTION 2F

SEWER JUNCTION 3F

NIOBE IS PINNED DOWN!

Move around the bottom level of the sewer junction and take out the SWAT guys, using collected Submachine Guns to eliminate enemies across the room who may be trying to sneak up behind Captain Niobe. Look for a **Health Pack** near some stairs on the side of the area if Neo catches a few scratches in the process.

SEWER JUNCTION 4F

After Neo helps Niobe eliminate the SWAT team, the three Upgraded Agents drop to the ground around them. Take out the three Agents using Focus attacks, and try to stick close to Niobe. Do not let her face an Agent alone, since only Neo is capable of eliminating one. Once your strikes begin to connect, use Focus to extend your combo and take it as far as it can go. By this point in the game, Neo has had enough skill upgrades that he should be able to take out an Upgraded Agent with one extended combo in Easy and Normal modes.

When the three are defeated, they possess new bodies on the top level. Leave Niobe on the ground floor and race up the stairs to the second level. Defeat all SWAT on the level, and be wary of Agents dropping granite from overhead. The boulders destroy large enough portions of the midlevel that Neo must use Focus Jumps to cross them. The SWAT emanate from an open doorway on the side. Close the door and cut off the SWAT team's entry point by striking the gears to the left of the archway. The other option is to use Focus and select the doors as targetable objects.

When 2F is clear, proceed upstairs to 3F and repeat the process. Collect Health Packs on 2F and 3F to regain lost life if needed. Then proceed up to 3F and take on the three Upgraded Agents once again. One of the best ways to kill the Agents is to knock them off the edge. This can be done at any time and is a fantastic advantage for Neo.

After the three Agents are defeated, wait for Niobe to join Neo on the top floor near the archway.

UPGRADED AGENTS

CLASS:	
	AGENT

SPECIAL ABILITIES:	
	BULLET DODGE
	POSSESSION
	FIST BOUQUET

The Path of Neo

Rescuing Niobe unlocks an ultimate finishing move, Killing Blow Level 3. When charged up and released, the move allows Neo to eliminate multiple enemies surrounding him or standing in a row. The Killing Blow changes depending on whether Neo is equipped with a melee weapon.

CAPTAINS' RESCUE: RESCUE MORPHEUS & TRINITY

OBJECTIVES

Rescue Morpheus & Trinity. Lead them to their exit:
- Get down to the street; protect Trinity & Morpheus.

- Lead Trinity & Morpheus to the exit.

- Destroy the helicopter.

OPPONENTS

Riot Police   SWAT

Soldier, Heavy Weapons

AVAILABLE WEAPONS

SMG   Assault Rifle

Grenade Launcher

STAGE MAP

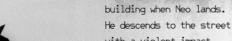

ZONE MAP

HEAVY FIREPOWER

Move to the edge of the building when Neo lands. He descends to the street with a violent impact, spreading the SWAT officers who have Morpheus and Trinity pinned. Quickly eliminate the remaining SWAT and collect their weapons.

A Heavy Weapons soldier with a Grenade Launcher has Morpheus and Trinity pinned down near their wrecked vehicle, and they cannot reach the exit. Neo can clear the path for them, but it requires a fairly specific route and good use of cover. Use Focus to run around the corner and down the street. Cross the street and take cover behind the large green dumpster on the opposite side.

Look back across the street to spot a sniper on a high platform. Take him down with gunfire.

RAISED PERCH

Now use Focus to race across the street to the base of the building where the sniper was perched. Move around the corner and Wall Run up the fenced area. Jump at the top of the run to grab the ledge overhead, where a **Health Pack** lies.

Go around the corner of the ledge, and Wall Run straight up. Jump at the top of the run and grab the next ledge up. Hidden on this ledge are a **Grenade Launcher** and a **Briefcase** that unlocks a secret when the level is completed!

From this high position, target and shoot the enemies at the end of the street. When Morpheus and Trinity begin to move up the avenue, drop from the building and join them.

OUTPOURING OF SWAT

More enemies emanate from the building to the left of Trinity and Morpheus' new location. Take down the SWAT team and start heading down the street. Riot Police with shields emerge from the starting point of the level. Use the Grenade Launcher to take them down easily as a cluster.

HELICOPTER ATTACK!

An Agent takes over the helicopter and attacks. Equip the Grenade Launcher and move toward the chopper. When the bird swoops in low to fire, shoot it from medium to short range. Two or three direct hits should do the trick.

Unlock Level Studies!

Collect the briefcase located on the raised ledge as described in the walkthrough section earlier to unlock a new gallery in the Media Viewer. These pieces include drawings and paintings created by the level designers to give the geometry modelers something to go by.

The Path of Neo

Saving Morpheus and Trinity from the firing squad unlocks the Aerial Killing Blow Level 2 ability. This Master Ability allows Neo to kick a foe several times from midair after charging up energy to attack.

CAPTAINS' RESCUE: RESCUE ROLAND

OBJECTIVES

Get Roland to the hard line.
- Find a way to block the SWAT units from entering the room.

- Use the crane to lift Roland to the upper level.

- Use the crane to take out the sniper in the Control Room.

OPPONENTS

Riot Police

Soldier

SWAT

AVAILABLE WEAPONS

Pistol

Shotgun

SMG

Assault Rifle

STAGE MAP

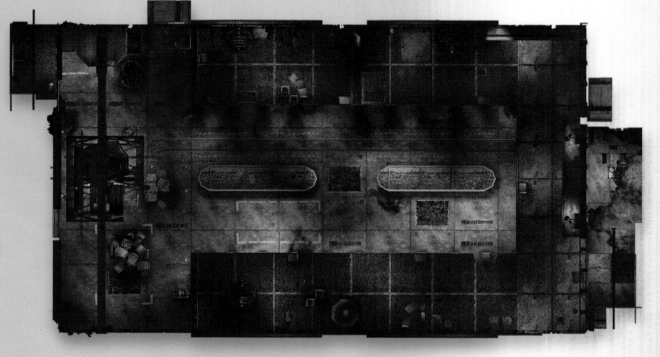

ROLAND NEEDS A BOOST

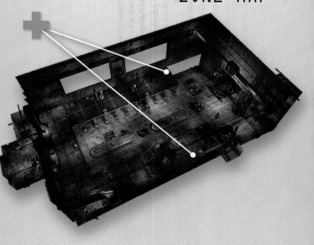

In order to reach the hard line, Roland needs Neo to lower the crane to the ground level so that he may board, and then he can be lifted to the upper level. The only way Roland will be safe during the process is if Neo clears the room of Soldiers and SWAT.

The enemies have taken up positions on both levels, and emanate from an open doorway on the bottom level. Notice the overloaded platform suspended high above the door. To prevent enemies from continuously entering the warehouse, use Focus to target the supports on the platform and shoot them. The load drops in front of the door, blocking access and killing any enemies in the path of destruction.

After taking out the enemies on the ground floor, double jump to the level above and kill the ones sniping from above. Use Antigravity or just head to one of the center tables and jump toward an area of the upper level where the balcony rail has been destroyed.

ZONE MAP

ZONE MAP

CODE VISION RULES!

Use Code Vision to detect several environmental traps that can be used to eliminate soldiers here. For instance, across the warehouse from Neo's starting point, an enemy stands under a bound stack of pipes. Use Focus to target and shoot the band holding the pipes to release them, killing the soldier below. To Neo's left there are a couple of enemies near an exploding barrel. Shoot the barrel to drop a heavy platform onto the soldiers. There are other exploding barrels around the room, and several electric generators. Throw or knock enemies into generators to send thousands of volts coursing through their bodies.

CRANE OPERATION

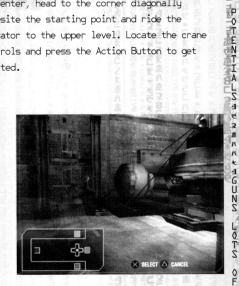

Once the room is clear of enemies and no more can enter, head to the corner diagonally opposite the starting point and ride the elevator to the upper level. Locate the crane controls and press the Action Button to get started.

The camera angle changes to view the entire warehouse, and a control diagram appears in the lower left corner of the screen. First, choose the green square in the diagram and press Select. The crane winch lowers the platform, allowing Roland to get onboard. Then use the crane controls again and choose either the yellow or red squares to deliver Roland to the upper level. It doesn't matter which side.

UPPER LEVEL ASSAULT

As soon as Roland lands on the upper level, more enemies take position on the upper level. Double-jump from the crane control platform onto the upper level and protect Roland from the new enemies.

A Riot officer with a Grenade Launcher takes a position in the control room, and begins blasting the area. The sniper is too well protected to shoot. Take out the enemies emerging from the doors on either side of the control room and stay close to the wall below the window. This way, the sniper will not shoot Roland or Neo, and may even eliminate his own men!

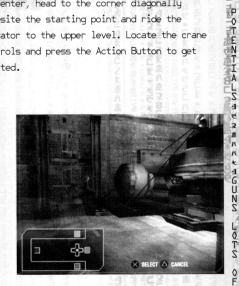

DESPERATE CRANE RETURN

Continue eliminating soldiers until Link calls on the phone. He hacks the crane controls so that it can be used as a weapon to eliminate the sniper. However, with enemies swarming the platform it is too dangerous to leave Roland to fend for himself while Neo rides the elevator.

From one corner of the upper level, Focus and Double-Jump toward the crane's cargo platform suspended in the center of the room. From there, Focus and double-jump over to the crane controls. Press the Action Button to use the controls, select the new white square on the control diagram and press Select to send the cargo smashing into the control room. Then jump back to the upper level and help Roland mop up the remaining Soldiers and Riot Police. This is quite a tough battle, and could take a few tries to clear!

The Path of Neo

For risking his hide to save Roland's, Neo unlocks the potential Weapon Strip Level 3 ability, making the upgrade available on the Path. During Weapon Strip, this upgrade allows Neo to grab enemies and use the weapons they hold against other foes. The form of the move changes depending on what type of weapon the target is brandishing.

THE WACHOWSKI BROTHERS' VISION

Here the player utilizes their skills and abilities against the upgrades. After the Agents are defeated, the player will have to protect the fleeing captains by flying through the canyons of the city, as they encounter heavy pursuit from the Agents and swarming, jack-booted, SWAT teams, who have also been upgraded.

This level could be broken into two levels, with the first one being above ground in the streets and alleys of Mega City, then below the surface, in the sewers, garages and waterways.

FILM FOOTAGE

The last human city. The lovers. The kid. "Is he here?"

This time however,
if any of the Captains' health bars reach zero, the game is over. "If one fails, all fail."

4

SERAPH'S APOLOGY

"You do not truly know someone until you fight them."
- Seraph

OBJECTIVES

Pass Seraph's test of your heart's resolve.

OPPONENT

Seraph (BOSS)

AVAILABLE WEAPONS

Broom   Mop

TEAHOUSE

CHINATOWN

THEATER

The Oracle's guardian must fight Neo in order to determine whether he is suitable to pass. But unlike the film, the battle is not relegated just to the teahouse. This is a super boss fight that spans three stages! Each location represents a trial, wherein Seraph attacks with a different fighting style.

Seraph uses Killing Blows and Super Jump attacks, much like Agents. He can also Wall Run, Wall Jump and perform other superhuman feats. In the teahouse, fight him as you would an Agent, by evading his blows with the aid of Focus and surprise attack him from behind. Inflict maximum damage by chaining together a combo that won't quit.

The first battle in the teahouse is actually not as hard as what is to come. Seraph smashes through the teahouse roof into Chinatown. There, he and Neo land on poles erected over a square that soon begins to burn. Use the Evade Button to leap from pole to pole, and the Movement Control to guide your direction. While standing on a pole near Seraph, press the Strike Button to leap at him and kick. The idea is to stun Seraph with kicks, and then press the Special Attack Button to throw him into the burning square below, inflicting damage. As time passes, the flames

in the square burn hotter, and many of the poles collapse, reducing the playing field. Continue kicking and flipping Seraph into the flames until his meter is depleted once again.

The battle then crashes onto the stage of a local movie house, where the famous fight scene with Seraph from The Matrix Reloaded is playing on the screen. Use Focus plus Evade moves to avoid Seraph's initial attack, and scoop up the Broom on the side of the stage. Use staff combos to attack Seraph. Seraph could possibly pick up a Broom or Mop of his own and counterattack.

The battle finally returns to the teahouse where it all started. Make use of Aerial Killing Blows and Focus attacks to drive his life gauge down as swiftly as possible. Seraph's life regenerates over time, so do not allow him too much downtime between Neo's extended combo attacks. Continue pounding Seraph until he accepts that Neo is the One.

SERAPH

CLASS:

EXILE

SPECIAL ABILITIES:

KILLING BLOW

MARTIAL ARTS COMBO ATTACKS

POLE FIGHTING

Unlock The Beginning of the End Combo!

When Seraph and Neo return to the teahouse for the final stage of their fight, destroy all eight support columns in the room and any one of the tables. Try positioning the support beams  between Neo and Seraph to see if your adversary can help you obliterate all eight. When this condition is fulfilled, a Briefcase appears in the center of the area. Pick it up and complete the level to unlock the Beginning of the End Combo. View this combo in the Extras Menu to learn how to bring your opponents to the brink of death instantly!

The Path of Neo

For defeating Seraph, Neo unlocks the possible upgrade, Aerial Killing Blow Level 3. This upgrade allows Neo to inflict the highest possible damage with an airborne attack, and also flings an enemy extremely far across areas, severely hurting any other foes they happen to collide with.

THE WACHOWSKI BROTHERS' VISION

To gain Seraph's trust, the player must defeat him in the teahouse as in the film. However, when Seraph's life meter reaches zero, Neo delivers a last crushing kick that hurls Seraph through the wall into the next store ladder factory.

Keeping the spirit of the teahouse, this will be a fight of balance in which the player will be penalized even perhaps lose, if they are thrown to or touch the ground. Again as Seraph's meter reaches zero, he is punched through the wall.

High above an open Chinese market. The player must hop from one tent pole to the next with the same objectives, beat Seraph and don't touch the ground. At some point the market catches on fire and the poles start to crumble, giving the player a time constraint.

The final environment is an empty movie theatre, where a lone, obese heckler sits watching The Matrix Reloaded. As the player fights Seraph, the teahouse fight is waged on the movie theater screen.

When the life meter reaches zero this time Seraph and Neo tumble into the screen itself returning to the teahouse atop the tables for the final round.

FILM FOOTAGE

The Oracle. Smith. Smiths.

The player
must withstand Seraph while a barrage of sharp rejoinders spews from the heckler ("Worst movie ever.")

THE BURLY BRAWL

"We're not here because we're free. We're here because we are not free. There's no escaping reason, no denying purpose. Because we both know that without purpose, we would not exist. It is purpose that created us. Purpose that connects us. Purpose that pulls us. That guides us. That drives us. It is purpose that defines us, purpose that binds us. We are here because of you, Mr. Anderson. We're here to take from you what you tried to take from us: Purpose."

- Smith

OBJECTIVES

Survive the onslaught of Smiths.

OPPONENT

Smith

AVAILABLE WEAPON

Burly Brawl Staff

STAGE MAP

TOO MANY SMITHS

Time to see what you have learned about multi-opponent combos. Strike one Smith, and then another and then press the Special Attack Button in combination with Focus to engage multi-opponent combos. Continue attacking one or two of the original Smiths until they expire. Smith quickly replicates himself to add more clones, so just continue striking Smiths in all directions. If things get too rough, Jump onto a Smith's head and use Focus along with the Movement Control to bounce from head to head. Move to the outside of the group and attack inward.

After the original Smiths are defeated, an army floods the courtyard. Time to get serious. Fight your way to the outside edge of the area and grab one of the **Burly Brawl Staves** out of the cement. Use staff combos to level groups of Smiths at a time. If health or Focus wane, use Evade moves to work your way out to the corners of the courtyard to collect **Health Packs** and **Focus Packs**.

SMITH BASEBALL

After defeating several Smiths with the Burly Brawl Staff, one of the buildings collapses under the weight of incoming Smiths. This is a clear indicator of how to reduce the number of Smiths. When facing one of the surrounding buildings, press the Special Attack Button and then the Strike Button to whack a Smith out of the ballpark, right into a building. When enough Smiths have been sent flying toward a building, the structure collapses, cutting off the Smiths' entry point.

When all of the surrounding buildings have collapsed, the number of Smiths remaining is reduced to just those that surround Neo. Defeat them to clear this extremely challenging stage.

Unlock The One Combo!

Defeat thirty Smiths during the Burly Brawl, and a Briefcase appears in the center of the courtyard area. Collect it and complete the level to unlock The One combo. Triggered by combining a complex series of moves, this combo can be viewed in the Extras Menu.

The Path of Neo

Taking on an army of Smiths and surviving improves Neo's abilities. The Focus Aerial Throw Level 3 upgrade becomes available on the Path of Neo. With this skill, Neo can now lift opponents into the air, spin them around and fling them into environmental objects, similar to the Tornado Throw move.

THE WACHOWSKI BROTHERS' VISION

The Burly Brawl should be by design the second longest fight in the game with a sense of escalation toward the impossible. Pedestrians and bystanders that wander into the action will be absorbed by Smith unless the player can stop him.

Only the most ardent player should outperform Neo and win in the end. Progressively the courtyard should crumble around the fight, the buildings riddled like Swiss cheese, against the Smith human cannonballs that hurtle from Neo's fists.

When the last Smith is defeated, the four buildings collapse, Neo standing in the courtyard center.

FILM FOOTAGE

Gods. Lust. The game.

SHINY'S COMMENTARY

Our programmers took this scene as one of their main challenges. How to get dozens and dozens of Smiths on screen at once?

One of the programmers, Martin Jensen, took this as a personal challenge, and eventually got a jaw-dropping 1,500 characters animating on screen at once.

THE FRENCHMAN

"[The Key Maker] disappeared. We didn't know what happened to him until now. He's being held prisoner by a very dangerous program, one of the oldest of us. He is called the Merovingian."
- The Oracle

OBJECTIVES

Defeat all the Merovingian's minions.

Escape the Chateau.

OPPONENTS

Vamp

AVAILABLE WEAPONS

Kama

Katana

Machete

Forked Sword

STAGE MAP

ZONE MAP

UNDER MERV'S WATCHFUL EYE

True to the films, the Merovingian's underlings prepare to saturate Neo with bullets. Stand your ground, press and hold the Focus Button and then press Evade to perform a Bullet Stop. When the Vamps move in to engage Neo in hand-to-hand, entertain them for a moment. But as soon as you are able to manage, leap over onto one of the stairwells and press the Action Button to pull a melee weapon off the wall. Use any variety of sword to hack the Merovingian's lapdogs to pieces. You remember your sword combos from back in the training days, right?

FIND THE DUNGEON

Facing the area under the balcony, head through the door on Neo's left. Follow the corridor into the library, where a secret door has been left open. Follow the stone passage down into the dungeon.

ZONE MAP

CORRIDORS OF ANGUISH

Head down the long central passage. Use weapons in Neo's possession to eliminate the Vamps and Dobermen that emerge from the rooms to either side and attack.

Upon reaching the large red cross at the end, head to Neo's right and follow the corridor to the end to find a **Briefcase**. Collect this item and complete the level to unlock a new bonus.

THE ROGUE WITCH

After collecting the bonus briefcase, head back in the opposite direction and use the Action Button to try to open the gate. A Vamp smashes through the wall and tackles Neo into a torture chamber. Use melee weapons to kill at least one of the Vamps.

ZONE MAP

Suddenly, the victim on the table unleashes a psychic scream that kills the two remaining enemies. Follow the Rogue Witch into the next passageway, and proceed down the corridor until Neo stands before three doors. The Merovingian obviously intends to see Neo jump through some hoops before he allows the One to escape.

Unlock Storyboard Sequence 2!

Collect the Briefcase lying near the gate at the end of the passage in the dungeon level, and then complete the level to unlock a second storyboard sequence on the Making Of screen.

DISTORTED DIMENSIONS

> **"Choice is an illusion** created by those with power, and those without."
> - The Merovingian

OBJECTIVES

Escape the Merovingian's Chateau:
-Find the right door.

OPPONENTS

Insectoids

AVAILABLE WEAPON

Candelabra

STAGE MAP

ZONE MAP

FACE ONE

Proceed to the end of the first corridor and open the door at the end to see the Merovingian's first challenge for Neo. The entire level is a giant surrealist puzzle, inspired in design by the paintings and sketches of M.C. Escher. The level has six 'faces'. To find the exit, Neo must travel from face to face by finding a magic door to transport him between faces and adjust the gravity. However, there are also false doors that may teleport him to undesirable locations.

Leap from the entrance over to the main platform. Ascend the stairs to the upper level to collect a burning Candelabra, which is an important weapon to have handy in this level. Then drop back down to the ground level and follow the passage with windows to a door. Open the door to be transported to Face 2.

ZONE MAP

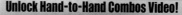

Unlock Hand-to-Hand Combos Video!

The Merovingian's surrealist nightmare level is also the home of several hidden briefcases, each unlocking a special feature of the Extras Menu. To find the first, approach the wall covered with windows and Wall Run up onto the top edge. Look across the chasm to spot a Focus Pack. Leap over to the Focus Pack's location, and then look to Neo's left. Jump into the square hole raised in the stone wall to find a Briefcase. Complete the level to unlock a video in the Making Of screen depicting many of Neo's impressive unarmed attacks.

FACE TWO

After another encounter with the surly Rogue Witch, Neo encounters a new type of enemy program. Insectoids are impervious to all attacks, but they are weak against fire. Use a burning Candelabra against them as a staff.

There are several of these located in the area. Insectoids can dissipate into red clouds. They then relocate instantaneously and reform, usually directly behind Neo if they can manage. Strike an Insectoid with a Candelabra while it is in red cloud form to kill it instantly!

Insectoids have a spinning Aerial Killing Blow attack whereupon they leap into the air, spin for a second and then launch at Neo. Turn this attack against them by using Bullet Stop (Focus + Evade) to prevent this attack, and press the Fire Button to make the Insectoid disperse into a red cloud.

Having slain the Insectoid, hop onto either of the large square platforms and follow the spiral stairs to the upper level. Collect Health Packs and Focus Packs by leaping to distant platforms if needed. On the top level, face the three doors in a row on a single wall. Go through the door on the right.

Unlock Storyboard Sequence 3!

Proceed to the upper level where the three doors are set into the wall. Use telekinesis (Focus + Evade) to remove the block from the pressure pad. Stand on the pad to open the wrought-iron gate blocking the center door. Quickly run through the center door. Neo reappears in a niche on a sideways face nearby.

Turn to Neo's left and jump up to the ledge. Follow the ledge to the end, and then Focus Jump across the gap to a platform where a Focus Pack sits. Turn around until you spot a Briefcase sitting on the very thin, inside ledge of a sideways arch. Jump over to grab the Briefcase, and then hold onto it until the end of the level to unlock the Storyboard Sequence 3 in the Making Of screen!

ENDLESS
CHAMBERS
ANGLE 1

ENDLESS
CHAMBERS
ANGLE 2

FACE 3

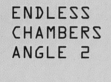

Defeat the twin Insectoids using a Candelabra and also the burning chandelier in the center of the area. Try to knock the Instectoids into the flame to destroy them.

To proceed, return to the door through which Neo entered this area. Wall Run up the wall to reach a flat area. Head to the right, and follow the back edge of the area until you can see a staircase going down. Follow this staircase to a door. Open that door to proceed.

Unlock Storyboard Sequence 4!

Immediately after reaching Face 3, go forward and drop from the ledge. Drop two more times, until Neo stands on a thin strip of stone. Then turn right and head to the edge of the platform. Turn left and walk off the edge to drop onto a platform below. Now turn around and face the opposite direction, and walk off the edge to find a Briefcase. Clear the stage to unlock yet another storyboarding sequence in the Making Of screen.

Unlock Storyboard Sequence 5!

Immediately after reaching Face 3, go forward and drop from the ledge. Drop two more times, until Neo stands on a thin strip of stone. Continue across this level toward the stained glass window in the distance. Wall Run up the surface beside the stained glass, and jump up to the ledge. Follow this ledge to the left and around the corner. A Briefcase is in a little alcove back there. Complete the level after collecting the case to unlock the last Storyboard Sequence in the Making Of screen!

ZONE MAP

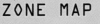

FACE 4

Descend the stairs and take on the Insectoids in the area below. Approach the gate to speak with the Rogue Witch, who finds herself trapped. Between fighting waves of Insectoids, use telekinesis (Focus + Evade) to lift the square block off of a pressure pad. Stand on the pad to release the Rogue Witch from the cage.

Continue fighting the Insectoids until the Rogue Witch figures out a way to open the gate for Neo. Once the gate is open, rush inside and go through the door on the left.

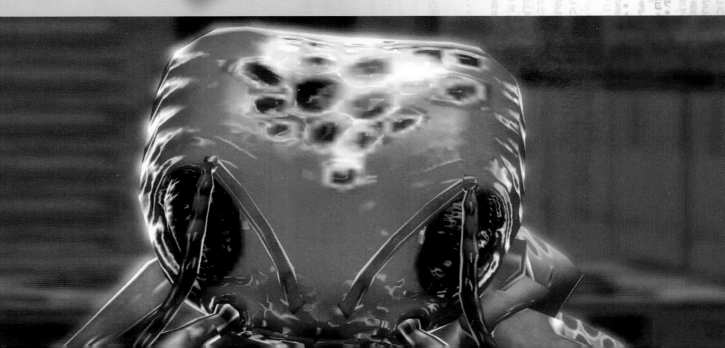

PATH OF THE ONE

ZONE MAP

ZONE MAP

ZONE MAP

ZONE MAP

FACE 6

Neo faces a choice between fighting a huge swarm of Insectoids or fleeing for the exit. To opt for the exit, jump across a series of cubes suspended in space toward a door. This actually turns out to be a fake door, but it teleports Neo to a new location directly in front of the exit door. Go through the door, and then head down the final corridor to the exit.

FACE 5

Many Insectoids surround Neo in an arena with a blazing central fire pit. In this instance, fight the Insectoids hand-to-hand and use throw moves to launch or flip them into the flames. New Insectoids keep appearing in this area, so move quickly toward the exit.

Take either staircase to the level above, and then turn around to see two doors on platforms hovering above the fire pit. Go through the door on the left to proceed to the final face.

DISTORTED DIMENSIONS

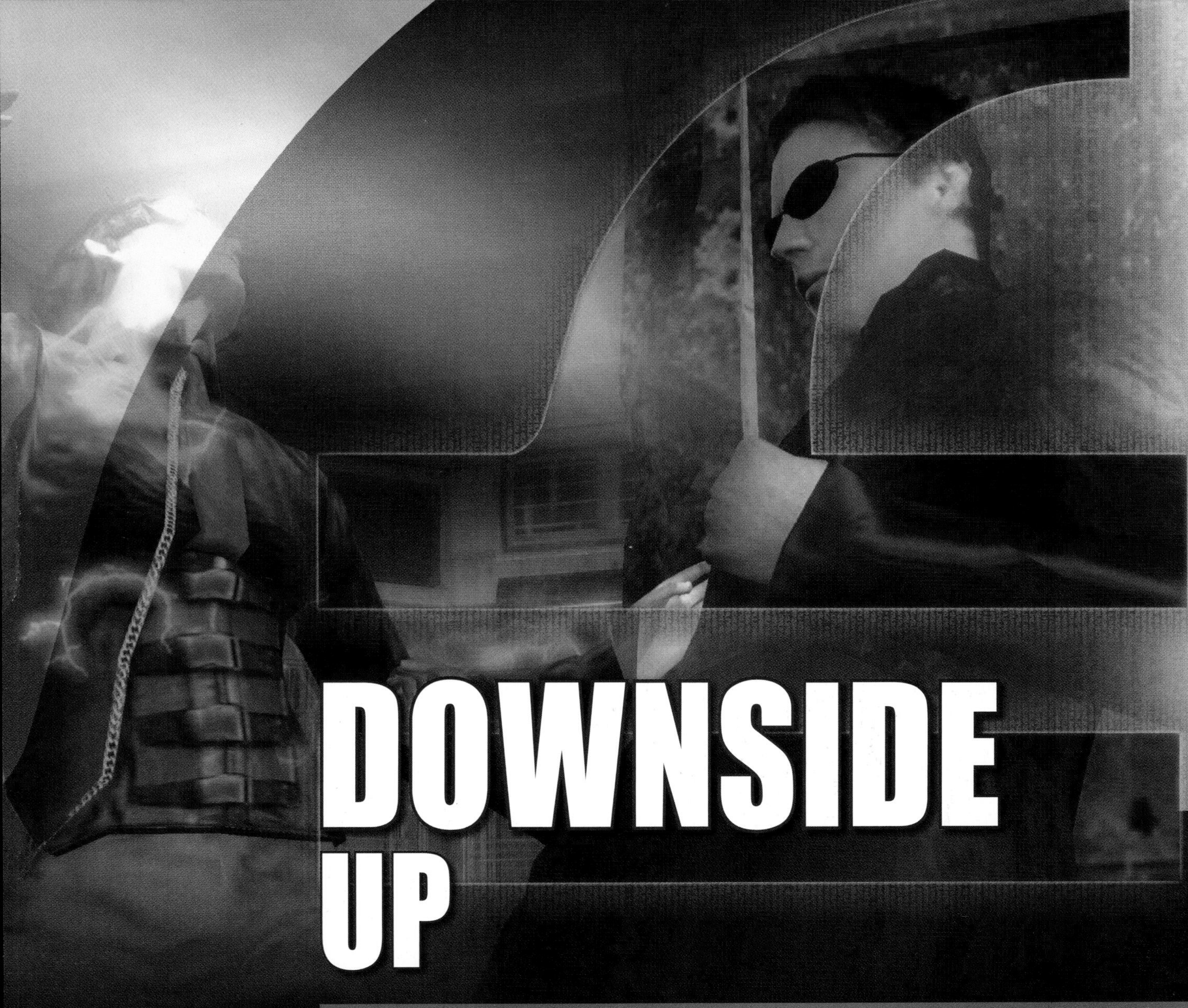

DOWNSIDE UP

> "These fellas work for my husband. They do his dirty work. They're very good, very loyal. They come from a much older version of the Matrix. But like so many back then, they caused more problems than they solved. My husband saved them because they are notoriously difficult to terminate."
>
> - Persephone

OBJECTIVES

Escape the Chateau:
- Eliminate all enemies.

OPPONENTS

Doberman   Vamp

Vamp Prime (BOSS)

AVAILABLE WEAPONS

Heavy Pistol   Shotgun   Sawed-Off Shotgun

SMG   Assault Rifle   Grenade Launcher

Flash-Bang Grenades

STAGE MAP

ZONE MAP

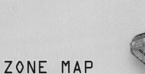

STRANGE INVITATION

Head down the passageway, collecting Heavy Pistols as you proceed. "Open" the doors and defeat the Dobermen and Vamps in the large room full of columns.

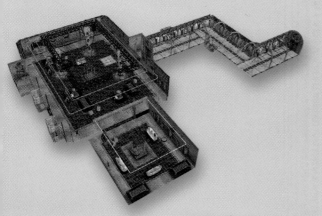

ZONE MAPS

ZONE MAPS

MYSTERIOUS ULTIMATUMS

Continue down the corridor and defeat the enemies encountered along the way. Smash into the next room and use armaments gathered to take out another group of Vamps and Dobermen. Continue down the next passage and up the green-lit stairs to yet another room full of challenges.

MAJOR SETBACK!

Defeat the enemies in the room. Be sure to Double-jump up to the center platform to pick up a **Grenade Launcher** in preparation for the upcoming boss battle. When all foes are defeated, some mysterious force returns Neo to the beginning of the stage!

THE EXPLODING COLUMNS

Head back through the corridor to the first chamber. Moving close to any of the columns in the room triggers the appearance of the Vamp Prime, who smashes out of a support as though it were some type of cocoon. Fight the fewest Vamps possible by working your way up the center of the room, defeating all of the Vamps that emerge from columns. Avoid moving around the room too much, or more Vamps may appear than Neo can handle!

Unlock Renderings Page 1!

Cause all of the columns in the antechamber to explode, and a Briefcase appears in the center of the room. Collect the case and complete the level to unlock a page of Renderings in the Media Viewer. There is need for caution, however. Avoid triggering too many column explosions at once, or the number of Vamps could quickly overwhelm Neo. Leave one Vamp alive at all times, and move toward two or three columns to trigger explosions. Defeat the present enemies down to the last, and then trigger

a few more column explosions to refresh the enemy numbers. Repeat this until all columns have burst and all enemies have been revealed and systematically eliminated.

TURN ON THE JUICE!

The Vamps in the torture chamber flip a switch, electrifying every metallic surface on the walls. Throw Vamps into the walls to eliminate them more quickly, but avoid allowing them to fling Neo there. Proceed down the final corridor to the two-level chamber.

VAMP PRIME

CLASS:

VAMP

SPECIAL ABILITIES:

HYPER EVADE

TELEPORT

Use a Grenade Launcher to soften up the leader of the Vamps. Then move in and engage him with extended combos. The Vamp Prime is capable of some fighting moves used by Dobermen, such as their claw attack, as well as strikes employed by Agents. He's a lithe, extremely mobile enemy, so use Evade moves to both keep away from him and avoid his attacks.

OBJECTIVES

Escape the Merovingian's Chateau:
- Choose the correct Exile.

- Defeat the Witch.

OPPONENT

Witch (BOSS)

AVAILABLE WEAPONS

Bo Staff	Katana
Morningstar	Spear
Sword	

THE WITCH

"Mark my words, boy, and mark them well. I have survived your predecessors, and I will survive you."
- The Merovingian

The Merovingian's psychic conjurer uses the Rogue Witch and the environment to her advantage. First, the Merovingian has constructed a little taste test for Neo. The Rogue Witch has been strapped to a table, and so have two clones that closely resemble her. Cross the room and choose one of the three Witches to protect. The real Rogue is usually the one on the left. But to be sure, use Neo's Code Vision. True to her nature, she is the one who is not asking for help. Stand between her and the Witch boss and use Bullet Stop to prevent the Rogue from being harmed. If you choose the wrong Rogue or fail to protect her with Bullet Stop, the Witch's attack reduces the Rogue's life to half, making it harder to protect her during the upcoming battle.

The Witch is an extremely tough boss, but she has discernable patterns that can be used against her. She attempts to use the Rogue Witch as a shield, and then utilizes telekinetic powers to pull the room apart and fling the pieces at Neo. If the Witch is standing in the open, use Bullet Stop (Focus + Evade) to freeze debris midair, then press Fire to fling it back at her. Avoid throwing the debris back if the Witch is using the Rogue as a shield.

The Witch proves extremely evasive most of the time, and uses Teleport to appear to teleport around the room. It is best to use Bullet Stop to reflect objects and pieces of debris back at her, and keep moving around the room in order to get close enough to go hand-to-hand, especially setting her up for longer, more powerful combos.

Once you have flung debris back at the Witch, she should be staggering slightly from the blow. Close the distance quickly and attack. Use one of the melee weapons hanging on the wall to damage the Witch. Otherwise, she is fairly impervious to barehanded attacks. She performs Teleport actions to relocate in the room, out of Neo's reach. Defend yourself from flying debris and go after her again.

If the Witch is hiding behind the Rogue, cross the room quickly and attack the Witch. Try not to strike the Rogue, since she proves to be a valuable ally later in the fight. If the Rogue Witch is killed, the battle continues but Neo must fight alone.

Continue fighting the purple Witch in this manner until half her life is depleted. She regenerates health, so do not be content to stand back and fight with telekinesis. When the Witch's health drops to 50 percent or less, The Rogue Witch finally breaks the spell she has been under. Now she fights alongside Neo, attacking the Witch.

At this point in the fight, the Witch changes tactics, becoming much more aggressive in hand-to-hand and with melee weapons, and unleashing special abilities to counter Neo's attacks. When a cloud of code appears around her, the Witch is able to counter all of Neo's hand-to-hand attacks, and render his melee weapons useless.

Time your attacks, and use a long weapon such as a staff, spear or morningstar to attack her. Use Special Attacks and Evades to stun the Witch, causing her defenses to drop. Try a Weapon Strip, or just beat her senseless with an extended combo or Killing Blow. Continue attacking her until she dies. The Rogue Witch makes this part of the challenge much easier if she is still alive.

WITCH

CLASS:

EXILE

SPECIAL ABILITIES:

HYPER EVADE
STAFF 360
STAFF THRUST
TELEKINESIS
TELEPORT

THE WACHOWSKI BROTHERS' VISION

The chateau fight should be a high flying aerial duel. And the player must be reliant as ever to their newly acquired skills in order to beat the gang of heavy metal goons. Side chambers may be revealed to widen the variety of weapons the player has to choose from.

After the fight is over, the Merovingian will smirk, assuring Neo that while he has bested his bodyguards he will not be able to defeat his "hounds."

When the door closes behind him, the player must race through the seemingly endless chambers of the chateau, fighting off the Merovingian's "hounds," a host of long forgotten root-programs - vampires; werewolves; witches and warlocks; leprechauns; ant-men; and big-headed aliens that carry ray-guns and intimidating-looking probes.

SHINY'S COMMENTARY

The Great Hall made another cameo appearance in Enter the Matrix. This time around, we would actually have a huge battle in it.

This is one of the prettiest levels in the entire game, with a large amount of great destruction effects.

Concept art for all of the "forgotten programs" characters was created, along with some character models. You can see an early version of the Leprechaun in the Zion Archives (an in-game unlockable).

TUNED OUT

"This level is filled with doors. These doors lead to many places. Hidden places."
- The Key Maker

OBJECTIVES

Rescue the Key Maker; protect Morpheus.

Find Morpheus and escape.

OPPONENT

Smith

STAGE MAP

TV LAND

Morpheus and Neo must escort the Key Maker through a series of surreal challenges created by the Smiths. Morpheus must remain unharmed as well, so stick close to him. Lead Morpheus through the corridor into the next chamber. Defeat a couple of low stamina Smiths. A wall disappears on the other side of the room, allowing the two to proceed.

ZONE MAP

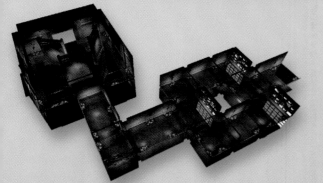

ZONE MAPS

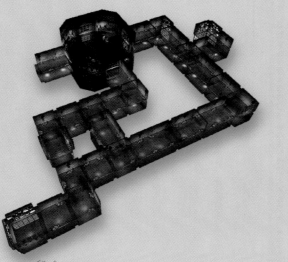

SUICIDE MISSION

When Morpheus decides to split up, follow his orders and head down the right branch in the path. Continue into the next room and avoid the exploding TVs flung by the Smiths. Fight and defeat the three Smiths to reveal the exit from the room. Use telekinesis (Force + Evade) to lift the TV sets in the room and fling them at the Smiths.

PROTECT THE KEY MAKER

Follow the maze of corridors. Smith appears on the monitors, telling Neo where to go. Oddly, you can trust him to lead you right back to the same room you were in previously. Only now, a group of Smiths is attempting to assimilate the Key Maker. Make your way over to the Key Maker and attack any Smith who is causing him damage. Continue protecting the Key Maker and attacking the Smiths until the group is eradicated.

WHERE IS MORPHEUS?

Follow the Key Maker into the escape corridor. Use Focus and Evade when moving through areas between monitors, because Smith causes the walls to explode. Continue leading the Key Maker down the corridor, taking out any Smiths that appear.

The top end of the corridor appears to be a dead end at first, but Morpheus soon creates a hole in the wall. Race forward to assist Morpheus against the Smiths. Unfortunately, Neo's mentor is flung through a magic door into another portion of the Matrix.

MINISTRY OF SMITHS

"All of our lives, we have fought this war. Tonight, I believe we can end it. Tonight is not an accident. There are no accidents. We have not come here by chance. I do not believe in chance."
- Morpheus

OBJECTIVES

Rescue Morpheus.

OPPONENT

Smith

AVAILABLE WEAPONS

Heavy Pistol   Sword

STAGE MAPS

FOYER

GROUND FLOOR

MEZZANINE

THE BEST DOOR

Move forward toward the doors, and collect the Swords from the statues on either side. Head into the chapel and defeat the three Smiths who stand ready for Neo. Then use the stairs to reach the mezzanine level and join Morpheus in his survival battle. Use additional Swords held by statues on the mezzanine level to defeat Smiths.

The Key Maker opens an exit on the bottom. Drop to the lower level and try to make it to the door, located in the corner near the chapel entry doors. The overwhelming number of Smiths makes it too dangerous to keep the door open, and so the Key Maker closes it. Soon, he opens another door up on the mezzanine level. The Smiths prove too thick for this exit too. However, the Key Maker drops Health Packs and Focus Packs near each door he opens.

Drop to the lower level and head toward the altar, where the Key Maker tries to open another door. Soon, he opens the door on the other side of the dais. Disengage from combating the Smiths and quickly run toward the Key Maker to escape.

Unlock Renderings Page 2!

Smash one of the Sword-holding statues on the mezzanine level to reveal a hidden Briefcase. The location is marked on the maps in this section. Collect the case and complete the level to unlock the second page of Renderings in the Media Viewer.

OBJECTIVES

Protect the Key Maker.

Get to the exit with the Key Maker and Morpheus.

Bonus Objective:
- Survive three waves of Smiths before exiting the level.

TAKING THE FLOOR

"Everything that has a beginning has an end. I see the end coming. I see the darkness spreading. I see death. And you are all that stands in his way."

- The Oracle

OPPONENT

Smith

AVAILABLE WEAPONS

Bo Staff

Flagpole

Assault Rifle

Grenade Launcher

STAGE MAP

VIDEO GAME VIOLENCE

Defeat two waves of Smiths using staff combos. The second wave carry Bo Staff weapons, so use Weapon Strip to acquire another staff after the integrity of the Flagpole gives out.

The Key Maker finally opens the door on the speaker's platform, only he does not find an exit. He does however find a **Grenade Launcher**, and hands it over to Neo.

The next wave of copies totes Assault Rifles. Drop to the floor and use the overturned tables as cover until the Smiths draw close. Then target clusters of Smiths and hit them with the Grenade Launcher. Continue that practice until the Grenade Launcher runs out of ammo, then switch back to Flagpole or Bo Staff and continue fighting the Smiths. When the Exile finally opens the door with the right key, join the Key Maker and Morpheus near the exit to complete the stage.

Unlock Character Concepts Page 2!

After the Key Maker finds the right key to create an exit, remain on the Senate floor and take out several additional waves of Smiths. The number required to unlock a bonus feature is specified in the Objectives screen, and changes depending on the difficulty level selected. Defeat the specified number of waves to unlock the second page of Character Concepts in the Media Viewer screen.

First wave defeated

THE WACHOWSKI BROTHERS' VISION

Before the Key Maker can run from the pressing Smiths in the industrial hall, a clutch of Smiths grab him and disappear through a portal. The player must stop the Smiths from absorbing Morpheus and the Key Maker, following them back and forth through the hidden trapdoors of the Matrix as they are under attack. These chases lead to--

• A television superstore, where the live in-store camera feeds pump images of Smith on the various-sized screens.

• An old church where a ministry of Smiths have surrounded a beaten down Morpheus.

• A glass and mirror supply house that is a breakable maze of reflections.

• On the Senate floor at the State of the Union address, where the player must escape with Morpheus before Smith can absorb the overwhelming number of politicians, spin doctors and cronies.

FILM FOOTAGE

The Architect. "Trinity!" "I believe in him." "Not impossible. Inevitable."

The siege. The Armada. A last kiss. "Peace."

SHINY'S COMMENTARY

We were concerned about gameplay in the thin Industrial Hall – the endless hallway of doors. The Wachowski Brothers solved the problem by focusing on the locations you can reach from the hall, rather than the hall itself.

The old church level, Ministry of Smiths, is another gorgeous level with tons of great destruction effects. The central statue collapse is a great effect, as the big marble angel s-l-o-w-l-y topples over.

MR. ANDERSON, WELCOME BACK

OBJECTIVES

Defeat Agent Smith.

OPPONENT

Smith (BOSS)

"Like what I've done with the place?"
-Smith

STAGE MAP

The titanic battle begins as do all previous battles, with two opponents fighting in the streets. Use an Evade move to avoid one of Smith's attacks, and then strike from the side or rear using Focus to improve timing and attack power.

Avoid falling into or being flung to the sidelines if possible. The Smiths surrounding the scene grab Neo and fling him back into the street, sometimes to a disadvantageous position. Continue fighting with Smith, combining Strikes with Special Attacks to trigger devastating combos. Try to keep him locked in place, pounding him with kicks or punches to drive his health meter down.

Do not worry about losing Focus. Focus recharges at a phenomenal rate, back to 100%. So just release the Focus Button for a second to recharge completely!

SMITH

CLASS:
> SMITH

SPECIAL ABILITIES:
> BULLET DODGE
> FIST BOUQUET
> KILLING BLOW

MR. ANDERSON, WELCOME BACK

Smith changes the rules of the game by taking the battle into the sky. Press and hold the Jump Button to fly at Smith, striking him on contact. Smith attempts the same attack. Avoid Smith's charge by pressing and holding the Evade Button. During a successful Evade, rapidly tap the Strike Button to perform a counter attack, stunning Smith and rendering him vulnerable to Killing Blows.

When Smith flies within range, use Strikes and then press Special Attack. Neo and Smith become locked in a flying struggle. Rapidly tap the Strike Button to break out of it and send Smith flying into one of the surrounding buildings. Fail to press the Strike Button rapidly enough, and it could be Neo sent flying into a building.

A Killing Blow properly executed immediately sends Smith into a building. However, if Smith counters Neo's Killing Blow with one of his own, the result causes a cinematic power bubble effect, spreading throughout the city like a tremendous wave. Continue attacking Smith until he is knocked inside a building.

STAGE MAP

Use focus to strike Smith a few times, then press Special Attack and engage him in the longest combo you can summon. Continue pounding Smith while Neo's feet are on the ground, and show him exactly who rules the Matrix.

PROGENY AND POTENTIALS GUNS LOTS OF GUNS WHAT IS THE MATRIX? EXTRAS UNLOCKING CHART PROGRAMS CONTROLLING PROGRAMS HMM UPGRADES PATH OF THE ONE

211

AERIAL BATTLE

"Why get up? Why keep fighting?
Do you believe you're fighting for something? For more
than your survival? Can you tell me what it is? Do you
even know? Is it freedom or truth? Perhaps peace? Could
it be love?"
- Smith

OBJECTIVES

Defeat Agent Smith.

OPPONENT

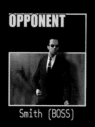

Smith (BOSS)

STAGE MAP

Continue using the flight controls to charge at Smith and knock him into surrounding buildings. When the duo floats past a building marked Kira Rowan Corporation, knock Smith into the structure for a little foot time.

On the ground, you should find Smith to be a bit more defensive and evasive. Continue using Focus for extended periods in order to Evade and counterstrike Smith's moves. If you manage to knock him off his feet, quickly summon a Killing Blow and unleash it as he rises and returns. Continue fighting Smith until his health is cut in half, at which point a cinematic occurs and Neo knocks Smith back into the sky.

Resume aerial fighting tactics, throwing Smith into buildings until his health is reduced to barely a sliver. Neo tackles Smith to the ground, creating an enormous crater.

Unlock Blur Cinematic Creation Video!

When fighting in the sky the first time, bash Smith and send him flying into the Kira Rowan Corporation building. Conversely, Smith can also knock Neo into the building to reach this point. A Briefcase lies on the floor. Pick up the case and clear the stage to unlock a video in the Movies screen depicting the creation process behind the MegaSmith introduction video, from concept to finished scene.

STAGE MAP

Neo immediately learns the Mega Punch Special Ability. Basically, this transforms the Killing Blow move into a cinematic that replicates the jaw-shattering punch Neo uses against Smith in <u>The Matrix Revolutions</u>.

Use Strikes to make Smith stagger, then press Special Attack and engage a long combo. Continue pummeling Smith until his life is cut in half or less, at which point a short "revenge" cinema plays and Smith knocks Neo into a wall. Smith then regains about half a life bar of health and continues. Evade Smith's attacks and use Focus to smash him into the surrounding crater walls. Whether the Mega Punch is used to finish Smith or not is up to you, but it is not essential to clearing the stage.

AERIAL BATTLE

THIS IS MY WORLD

OBJECTIVES

Wait for the right time to charge Smith.

Defeat MegaSmith.

OPPONENT

MegaSmith (BOSS)

Smith has gone to enormous proportions to seek revenge against Neo. But although this battle may look difficult at first, it is really nothing more than a test of timing and strategy. Follow the advice in this column, and you should be able to bring MegaSmith crashing down without taking a single hit!

Neo floats in the air before MegaSmith. Surrounding the area are several partially collapsed building structures. Use the Movement Control to glide left or right, behind one of the structures. If MegaSmith attacks and strikes one of the structures, he begins to roar and throws his hands up. This is when MegaSmith is vulnerable. Press and hold the Jump Button to make Neo charge forward and shoot through MegaSmith like a bullet, taking out a large chunk of its structure. After a dozen or so hits are inflicted in such a manner, MegaSmith is crippled to the point where it can no longer fight and the battle is over.

MEGASMITH

Learn to identify MegaSmith's attack patterns, so that you can evade them properly. When MegaSmith raises both hands slightly, it means he is going to clap them in an attempt to strike Neo. Tilt the Movement Control left or right and press Evade to soar out of harm's way. When MegaSmith dips one of his shoulders, he is about to bring his arm up in an uppercut. This too can be evaded by soaring to either side.

When MegaSmith crosses his arm over his body, it means he is about to perform a backhand blow. The only way to avoid this attack, unless you can take shelter behind a building, is to perform a vertical Evade. Stop moving completely, and then press and hold the Evade Button to soar straight up. Do not hesitate; perform this move as soon as MegaSmith crosses its arm in front of its torso. If Neo evades several attacks in a row, this can trigger MegaSmith's rage and he becomes vulnerable.

After MegaSmith suffers two or three of Neo's attacks, each of his subsequent arm waves sends a cluster of Smiths flying at Neo. Evade to the left or right, repeatedly if needed, to avoid the flying Smiths. If one of the Smiths grabs Neo, rapidly tap the Strike Button to break free. If Neo is tied up with a flying Smith, he may be unable to evade MegaSmith's direct attacks.

If MegaSmith should happen to slap Neo, the hero could be knocked all the way to the end of the block. MegaSmith tears up chunks of macadam and hurls them at Neo. Although it is possible to evade the flying garbage, doing so is also trickier and more dangerous. Instead, remain in the middle of the street. When MegaSmith hurls debris, wait until the projectile rises to the top of the screen. Then hold Focus and Special Attack to charge up a Killing Blow. Release the buttons when the debris is about to strike, and Neo smashes the debris into a million bits. Continue smashing flying debris until MegaSmith becomes frustrated and screams in rage. Then press and hold the Jump Button to attack MegaSmith and return to the aerial battlefield. Repeat all aforementioned strategies until MegaSmith is defeated. Congratulations, you just freed the Matrix!

THE WACHOWSKI BROTHERS' VISION

The final brawl between Neo and Agent Smith should have the destructive capacity as any Japanese monster film. Streets will ripple, walls will detonate and buildings will topple under the onslaught of the fight.

The gamepath will follow a similar progression as the film; from street, to canyon, to building, to sky, to crater.

A rumbling shakes the crater, when suddenly, the ground explodes and MegaSmith tears up from the depths.

The last section of gameplay pits the player against a thirty story tall, fire-breathing Smith. At close up it is apparent that MegaSmith is made up of thousands of the normal sized Smiths. If the player is able to deliver significant chunks of damage to MegaSmith, Smith's should shake from his body like sprays of blood.

When at last MegaSmith is beaten, the player will either get an incredible visual animatic that explains their path to higher consciousness ... or a medal.

The end.

SHINY'S COMMENTARY

The progression described - street, canyon, building, sky, crater - became Shiny's shorthand names for all of these level sections.

The MegaSmith sequence was created by FX studio Blur, based on the storyboards by Shiny's Cinematic Co-Director, W.D. Hogan.

Blur is responsible for some of the coolest cinematic sequences seen in videogames today, and the MegaSmith sequence is simply awesome. Every time we had a viewing at Shiny, we cranked up the speakers and a huge crowd would gather.

EXTRAS UNLOCKING CHART

Although covered more thoroughly in the **Path of the One** chapter, here is a handy reference chart that shows how all locked secrets in the Extras Menu are unlocked, based on type.

MOVIES

Each movie montage becomes unlocked in the Movies screen after it is viewed during the course of the game.

SPECIAL COMBOS

	COMBO	DESCRIPTION	STAGE	CONDITION
	THE CODE BREAKER	Focus + Special Attack, Rapidly Tap Strike, Special Attack, Rapidly Tap Strike	Weapon Training	Find the Briefcase among the Operator's secret stash in the upstairs corridor, when returning to teahouse. Clear the stage.
	QUICK KICKS	Strike x4, Focus + Strike, Special Attack + Strike	Storming the Drain	In the second to last room, touch the top two platforms in the room and clear the stage.
	MACHINE GUN KICK	Strike x5, Focus + Strike, Special Attack + Strike, Rapidly Tap Strike	The Chase: "I Need an Exit!"	Find the Briefcase in the corner of the market area behind the fruit stands. Clear the stage.
	ULTIMATE HYPER STRIKE	Strike x4, Focus + Strike, Special Attack + Strike, Focus + Special Attack, Strike	Redpill Rescue: The Security Guard	Defeat the SWAT team on the stairs in the given time limit and clear the stage.
	THE BEGINNING OF THE END	Strike x4, Focus + Strike, Special Attack + Strike, Focus + Special Attack, Rapidly Tap Strike	Seraph's Apology	After returning to the teahouse from the theater, destroy one of the tables and all eight support columns in the room. Pick up the Briefcase appearing in the center of the level. Clear the stage.
	THE ONE	Strike x5, Focus + Strike, Special Attack + Strike, Rapidly Tap Strike, Focus + Special Attack, Rapidly Tap Strike, Special Attack, Rapidly Tap Strike, press Jump as Neo preps uppercut, Spin Movement Control 360 degrees at peak of jump	The Burly Brawl	Defeat 30 Smiths. A Briefcase appears in the center of the level. Pick it up and clear the stage.

MEDIA VIEWER

MEDIA	DESCRIPTION	STAGE	CONDITION
LEVEL CONCEPTS	Rendered and painted artwork used to sketch levels.	He's Heading for the Street	Reach Trinity at the 1st floor exit.
CHARACTER CONCEPTS (PART 1)	Renderings and paintings of in-game and unused characters.	Dojo Training	Finish all training programs.
CHARACTER CONCEPTS (PART 2)	Renderings and paintings of in-game and unused characters.	Taking the Floor	Defeat several waves of Smiths after the Key Maker opens the exit.
LEVEL STUDIES	Renderings and paintings of in-game and unused characters.	Captains' Rescue: Morpheus & Trinity	Collect the Briefcase on the high ledge and clear the level.
RENDERINGS (PART 1)	Renderings of in-game models and weapons.	Downside Up	Trigger all of the exploding columns in the antechamber. A Briefcase appears in the center of the room. Pick it up and clear the stage.
RENDERINGS (PART 2)	Renderings of in-game models and weapons.	Ministry of Smiths	Smash a statue on the upper level to reveal a Briefcase. From the entrance, the statue is upstairs to the right. Clear the level.

CHEATS

	CHEAT	DESCRIPTION	STAGE
	LOTS OF GUNS	Additional weapons are loaded near the starting point of every stage.	Beat the game on any mode, Novice/Master/The One.
	INDESTRUCTIBLE MELEE WEAPONS	Melee weapons never break.	Beat the game on any mode, Novice/Master/The One.
	VAMPIRIC REGENERATION	Neo regains health by defeating enemies. The amount of healing is dependent on the enemy type defeated.	Beat the game on Master or The One mode.
	UNLIMITED AMMO	When a gun runs out of ammo, Neo suddenly has more.	Beat the game on Master or The One mode.
	REFLECT BULLETS	Bullets do not cause damage to Neo. Melee weapons and hand-to-hand attacks still cause damage.	Beat the game on The One mode.
	UNLIMITED HEALTH	Health never decreases.	Beat the game on The One mode.

THE MAKING OF...

VIDEO	DESCRIPTION	STAGE	CONDITION
STORYBOARD SEQUENCE 1	Depicts the scene at the beginning of the Captain's Rescue stage, comparing animated storyboards to finished video.	Redpill Rescue: The Key	Clear the stage without using weapons.
STORYBOARD SEQUENCE 2	Depicts the scene at the beginning of the Weapon Training stage, comparing animated storyboards to finished video.	The Frenchman	At the end of the Dungeon Hallway, go to the right and follow the passage to the end. Pick up the Briefcase near the gate. Clear the stage.
STORYBOARD SEQUENCE 3	Depicts the scene at the beginning of the Rooftop Assault stage, comparing animated storyboards to finished video.	Distorted Dimensions	On Face 2, move the block near the three doors to reveal a pressure pad. Stand on the pad to open the gates on the center door. Quickly enter the door. Neo is teleported to a small nook. Turn to the left and jump onto the ledge above. Follow the ledge to the end, and jump across the chasm to a Focus Pack. Turn to the right and look at the back side of the stone wall to see a Briefcase lying on the edge of a sideways arch. Collect the case and clear the stage.
STORYBOARD SEQUENCE 4	Depicts the scene at the end of the Subway Showdown stage, comparing animated storyboards to finished video.	Distorted Dimensions	On Face 3, move straight ahead from the entrance to the edge of the platform and drop to the level below. Continue dropping to a series of sideways arches. Head to the right and then drop to the level below to find a Briefcase in a niche. Clear the stage.
STORYBOARD SEQUENCE 5	Depicts Neo's descent scene during the Captains' Rescue: Morpheus & Trinity stage, comparing animated storyboards to finished video.	Distorted Dimensions	On Face 3, move straight ahead from the entrance to the edge of the platform and drop to the level below. Continue dropping to a series of sideways arches. Head across the stage toward the stained glass window. Wall Run up the surface beside the stained glass, and follow the ledge to the left. At the corner, go behind the wall to find a small alcove hiding a Briefcase. Clear the stage.
VIEW STAFF COMBOS	A video showcasing Neo's staff weapon combinations.	Kung Fu Training	Execute 3 Silent Takedowns on all three enemies in the tool shop, then collect the Briefcase that appears near the alarm. Clear the level.
VIEW SWORD COMBOS	A video showcasing Neo's sword weapon combinations.	Sword Training	Smash the pots behind the waterfall to reveal a Briefcase. Clear the level.
VIEW HAND-TO-HAND COMBOS	A video showcasing Neo's martial arts combinations.	Distorted Dimensions	On Face 1, Wall Run up the wall with windows and look across the chasm. Jump to the Focus Pack's location, and look to the left. Jump into a raised square hole in the stone wall. Pick up the Briefcase located there, and clear the stage.

ADDITIONAL

ITEM	DESCRIPTION	STAGE	CONDITION
MASTER MODE	Normal difficulty setting	Have You Ever Had a Dream, Neo?	Defeat the first wave of foes.
THE ONE MODE	Hard difficulty setting	Have You Ever Had a Dream, Neo?	Defeat Agent Smith.
ZION ARCHIVES LEVEL	A stage containing player models cut from the final game. Available in the Level Select screen.	Redpill Rescue: The Security Guard	The Spoon Atman Principle becomes unlocked in the Path of Neo screen. Activate this principle to unlock the stage in the Level Select screen.
BLUR CINEMATIC DOCUMENTARY	A video depicting the process behind creating the final rendered cutscenes of the game. Viewable in the Making Of screen.	Aerial Battle	During the fight, when Neo and Smith float past the Kira Rowan building, knock Smith into the building or let Smith throw Neo into the building. Collect the briefcase lying on the floor, and clear the stage.